CYBER SEX

A Guide to Better Relationships through Anonymous Questions and Real Life Answers

SPENCER AND SHARONDA PARKER

Disclaimer: Upland Avenue Productions, LLC, and Spencer and Sharonda Parker make no representations or warranties with respect to the accuracy or completeness of the contents of this work and specifically disclaim all warranties, including without limitation warranties of fitness for a particular purpose. No warranty may be created or extended by sales or promotional materials. The advice and strategies contained herein may not be suitable for every situation. The work is sold with the understanding that the Publisher is not engaged in rendering legal, accounting, medical, therapy, or other professional services. The work is also sold with the understanding that the author is not engaged in rendering any kind of therapy or counseling services. If professional assistance is required, the services of a competent professional person should be sought. Neither the Publisher nor the Author shall be liable for damages arising therefrom. The fact that a website or organization is referred to in this work as a citation and/or a potential source of further information does not mean that Upland Avenue Productions, LLC, or Spencer and Sharonda Parker endorses the information or organization or website.

Cyber Sex: A Guide to Better Relationships through Anonymous Questions and Real Life Answers
ISBN-13: 978-0615926735
ISBN-10: 0615926738

CYBER SEX

Preface

Five years ago my husband and I started selling adult toys as a means to supplement our income. Never in a million years did we think we would be writing a book and owning one of the hottest adult toy stores in Louisiana. When you saw us you also saw our toys because we took them with us everywhere we went. What we soon found out was other couples were having standard sexual encounters. We were so open and free about our sex life, and most people we ran into were very private about their sex life. My husband and I honestly thought that everyone was having amazing sex, but we soon found out that people were in sexually starved relationships. We had this thing where we felt like we had to try the toys and products first before we could sell it. We felt like in order to give people our honest opinion we had to be the "test dummies".

After hosting fantasy parties we would talk one on one with the guest and some of their stories were heart breaking. We heard about how they would fake orgasms, how the men had problems with maintaining their erection, how some couples have never used a bullet and the list would go on and on. At that point we decided to take a different approach. We would host the fantasy parties but not only would we talk about the products and how to use them but we would also talk about some of the problems that couples were having in the bedroom, and how to solve those problems. We would explain why sexual satisfaction was so important in relationships and tell them why it was important to keep their bedroom fun and exciting.

One day in October of 2011, we took a childish game on a social networking site and turned it into a business opportunity. All we would do is answer anonymous questions about sex, relationship issues, fantasies and anything else you could think of. My husband would also give advice from a male's perspective so that the readers would see both points of view. That's how Questions and Answers were started and we haven't looked back since.

For instance, one reader asked the ultimate question. She said, "I have been reading your Q and A and you give really good advice. I am wondering what made you want to do this? It seems like you do a lot of research to be able to answer these questions so well! Very impressed!!!"

I confidently replied that I have been selling sex toys for five years. During that time people would ask for help and advice. I came to the conclusion that more people probably had questions but just was too afraid to ask. So I started posting the questions and answers so everyone could see them and learn. People started sending me letters and I would just give my opinion and I also allowed my readings to give their input. In my opinion sex is a beautiful thing and I just wanted to take a subject matter that most people frown upon and bring a positive light on it. I'm glad you enjoy the page... And yes I'm always reading and doing research.

We decided to write a book because there was a demand for it. After hosting hundreds of Fantasy Parties, Oral Sex Classes, and talking to customers in the store we decided to give the public what they have been asking for. Our followers would log on everyday just to see what was posted so they could comment or share what we have posted. We have had people to tell us our page has saved their marriage, or has gotten them through their work day.

CHAPTER 1:

Benefits of a Healthy Sex Life

Sex is important in any healthy relationship. You have to remember the same things you did to get that person are the same things you have to do to keep them. It is also important to grow sexually. If you keep doing the same thing every time you and your partner have sex you both will soon be bored. You have to change it up, new positions, new location, new toy, or new lingerie, just keep each other's attention. Sex should be fun and exciting. It's something you should look forward to. You should make time for sex but it should not be planned. In other words you should be having sex on a regular basis but it shouldn't be scheduled with a date or time. Being spontaneous is what keeps the bedroom alive.

Next you have to take the time to get to know your partner and what turns them on. Every person is different and what works for one may not work for another. So don't assume you know what your partner likes. Talk to them and find out what they like and what their fantasies are. Remember to be open-minded and don't take things personal when a person tells you some things they want you to do different to please them.

We always hear people say, "I'm tired of doing the same old thing but I'm with someone who is not open to anything." In order for you and your partner to venture into another area you have to make sure both of you are comfortable with the whole idea. Start off slow with a romantic setting, some sexual games, and then move it up to a small stimulator. When you are dealing with someone who is closed minded about sex you have to do small things to open their minds up. Will you have to put in lots of work to get them where you want them sexually? Yes, but it will be worth it.

We don't think people visit their local sex shops enough. Some people have never been inside of an adult toy store and when they do visit it's for a bachelor/ bachelorette party or Valentine's Day. New products come out every month, and everything is designed to take your sex life to the next level. You should visit your local sex shop on a regular basis. The same way you visit your local grocery store and you go down all the isles to look and see what they have new, you should do the same thing at your local adult toy store. Don't be afraid to ask questions, and try something new.

QUESTIONS AND ANSWERS

Q: I want to do something nice sexy and romantic for my man.....any ideas?

A: Because you said romantic I will take it slow. You can give him a nice bath in some bath beads. This will help him relax. Light candles all over the bathroom and bedroom. Dry him off in a nice big plush towel and lay him in the bed. Blindfold him and take some silk scarves and tie him to the bed. Talk to him and tell him how much you love him. Get some massage candles and light them. Pour the warm soy wax all over his body and rub it in. When you get to his dick make sure you stroke it slow and complement him on how good it looks. You can insert a bullet inside you and then insert him in you. Don't turn the bullet on at first, wait a few seconds. He will be blindfolded and tied up the whole time. He should love it.

Q: I'm a big girl, but I'm not a lazy fuck. I have to enjoy it just as much as him. The next day everything is hurting, but why?

A: Sex is exercise, sometimes we use muscles that we haven't used in a while and we wake up sore. It's no different than working out. Once your body gets used to it you will be ok. Just take an over the counter pain pill. U will be ok.

Q: I have a question: My woman loves strippers, loves going to fun parties, and she loves going clubbing doing freaky dances but when she come to bed with her man she acts all shy and stuff. I would love for her to go down on me more often and do all kinds of freaky stuff. I just need her to be the aggressive one sometimes. If she loves me she should be willing to do what makes me happy. What should I do?

A: You have to show her what you want and tell her what you want. The bedroom should not be quiet. You have to let her know what feels good to you and let her know what you expect. If you like to get your dick sucked you need to say it but please be prepared to eat some pussy just as much. Tell her to shake that ass for you. Pick her ass up just like the strippers do her. If you can't lift her up, get a door swing that will help you support her weight if you can't hold her up. Keep in mind a closed mouth doesn't get fed.

Q: I am in need of some new things. My boyfriend was released a month ago from prison. He did 14 1/2 years and I have been trying and pulling out everything I got. I've been using lingerie and fishnets, handcuffs and blindfolds. I need some new inspiration to keep this man's attention. Can you PLEASE HELP!!!!!

A: If you want to keep his attention get spontaneous. Have sex in new places, perform lap dances in sexy lingerie, leave him love notes, and if you don't have couples toys you better get you some. Try bathing him with a vibrating sponge, and when he gets out dry him off and give him an erotic massage.

Q: Hey, It's me again! My hubby and I have been trying to conceive for about 11 yrs. We've been to a fertility doctor. They told us his sperm count is low but never said he couldn't produce. I have a 12 year old. Recently, when we have sex, I lay there because people say lay about 15 minutes to help the sperm get to the egg. When I don't get up to pee or take a bath I have this odor come, why? What's that about? All I want is to conceive, healthy preferably twins, any suggestions?

A: There are a few things you can try. A position pillow is an option. It will tilt your bottom upwards so the sperm shoots straight to the egg. Next, also maintaining a high protein, low-fat diet that is rich in vegetables and whole grains may help, as well. The timing of intercourse may impact a low sperm count, as well. Ejaculating less often, for example, is thought to help with low sperm count. It is thought that keeping at least three days between ejaculations is probably the range that you should go for. Avoiding excess heat on the testicles, as well, may be an important part of treatment for a low sperm count. This would include avoiding tight or restricting underwear or clothing, and avoiding saunas or hot tubs.

Q: Is it normal for a woman to have a higher sex drive than men? I want sex MORNING, NOON, AND NIGHT and ANYTIME IN BETWEEN but my man on the other hand wants to have sex once or twice a week. Don't get me wrong when we have sex it is awesome but I want more. Can you please give me some advice on what I can do?

A: You sound like you need to get him some help... meaning invest in a toy. Play with that pussy in front of him. Lol. I'm just playing. Sometimes we have to think outside of the box. New lingerie, Sexy Strip Tease, Role Playing, lots of teasing and touching. Just keep blowing his mind. Make him want you.

Q: My man says that I am a trip and he 'aint ever been with anybody like me. Well, I rape this man when he's sleep. I just have to have it. Sometimes his smell makes me want to lick and suck all on his sexy ass. Anyway, at night when he is asleep, I rub and suck on his neck and all that good shit. I suck his dick and he has no choice but to get that ass up and put the dick on me. He said he doesn't have an issue with me doing that but in his 40 years he hasn't had a woman rape him. I want to know am I the only female that rapes her dude. Is this normal or am I tripping?

A: Trust me; you're not the only female that takes that dick. He should be lucky to have you. You just keep on doing what you doing.

Q: Help a sister out. I would say twice a day I find myself thinking about my man outta the blue, and how he hit this, at work, driving down the road, sitting at home just anywhere. I can really feel him pushing inside of me but of course he is not really there. So I go into the bathroom (like I always do after we have sex) and my underwear feels like I just stepped out of a pool of water or a shower. I mean wet, wet all over myself. Is this normal for a woman or am I tripping? To be honest I know I am dick whipped. What is a girl supposed to do???

A: Are you serious? Do you know how many women would love to be in your shoes? That's what that Dumb Dick do to you. Have you daydreaming and shit. Pussy soaking wet 24/7. Shit I'm happy for you. What's a girl supposed to do? Enjoy every minute of it, keep smiling and keep that man happy!

Q: My boyfriend and I have been together for eight years and I haven't showed my nympho side to him yet. Well his birthday is Friday and I was wondering what I could do for him to get his day started off right. I want it to be spontaneous but sexy. I am willing to try anything.

A: Start the morning off with a strip tease, don't fuck him yet. Make him wait. If he has to go to work send him naked pictures throughout the day telling him how you can't wait to put that pussy on him the next time your eyes meet. Bathe in some glow bubbles so that when you walk into your dark room your whole body is glowing. When he cums swallow that shit. Job Done. Happy Birthday.

BENEFITS OF A HEALTHY RELATIONSHIP FROM A MALE'S PERSPECTIVE:

The greatest benefit of a healthy sex life is a healthy relationship. Men constantly talk about sex but rarely talk about their personal hang-ups and pitfalls in the bedroom. This is why it is very important to have open communication in the bedroom. You have to know what your partner likes and does not like. You have to be able to compromise and try new things, and there has to be a feeling of mutual respect and equality in the bedroom. These things are accomplished by talking to your partner about every aspect of your sex life. Discussing your fantasies, your fears, the things you want to try and the things you aren't willing to do in the bedroom. This gives your partner a map directly to your areas of maximum stimulation. It is also important for a man to be comfortable in the bedroom. An overly aggressive woman can be intimidating and can kill the mood in an instant because she made the man feel inadequate in some way. Ladies if you find yourself in a situation where your partner was ready and all of a sudden everything went south, the best thing you can do is be encouraging and supportive. Every man has had that moment when one head lost communication with the other. It may have been from the lack of desire, medical issues or even nervousness. Whatever the case may be, kind words and understanding will get things going back in the right direction. A healthy sex life can be very awkward at times but through communication, respect, and compromise (three things you will hear a lot about in the chapters to follow) you will begin to reap the rewards in no time.

CHAPTER 2:

Honesty and Communication

Being able to communicate with your partner honestly is very important in a relationship. You should not be afraid to tell your mate if you really enjoy your sexual experience with them or that you really feel like they need some work in the bedroom. When you communicate with them your feelings about such a touchy topic take into consideration they do have feelings to. Sometimes it's not what you say but it's how you say it. Communicate out of love not anger. Make sure you are communicating with your partner and not everyone else like family members or friends.

QUESTIONS AND ANSWERS

Q: I got a little part time boo-thang. How do I introduce him to my toy bag?

A: Shit, you know I believe in turning 'em out. Start off slow with some extreme foreplay. When he can't take any more put your bullet in between your teeth and put it on the head of his dick. He's going to love the vibration. Put the bullet inside of you and let him come in behind it. The next time pull out that Rabbit and tell him to fuck you with it.

Q: Good Morning Mrs. Parker. I have a real big problem. The man I'm dating loves the clubs. He goes Mondays, Wednesday, Thursdays, Fridays, Saturdays and Sundays. Now I'm asking him to spend time with me. It could either be a movie, out to eat or just something. Now if I plan something he has to stop by a club and get a drink before he picks me up. Ok, if I say come over and get some pussy it's no hesitation. I'm off of work every other weekend and I can be in the house not doing shit but call him and he's in the club. I'm sick of his shit and yes I raise hell and yell. What should I do?

A: Your man didn't get like this overnight. More than likely when you met him he was going out to the club. It seems to me he likes the night life and is the kind of person that always has to be doing something. Start to ignore his ass, don't call him, and don't ask him to do this or that. You get your own life and start doing the things you like to do. Men hate to be ignored. When he calls reject his ass. When he wants to fuck tell him you got plans. Make him miss you. Another thing is men hate nagging. So if he comes around and you're always nagging and complaining then he more than likely will not want to spend time with you. One thing I know is you want to spend time with what you love. The process might be painful but you have to get you a life. Join a book club, social club, etc. something to get your mind off of him.

Q: This is my problem, years ago when I was a child in middle school/high school I thought I was gay. People told it to me so much growing up I just started to believe it. I started hanging with gay people because they accepted me, but I would still sneak and look at females. Now that I'm an adult, I only want to date females but they all say the same thing "people say you are gay" and the relationship goes downhill from there. Have I ever had sex with a man? Yes. Have I ever been penetrated? No. Does this make what I did right? No. But I don't want to be in a relationship with a man. I really desire to be with a woman who will love me for me. I'm not bi-sexual because I am not attracted to men. My past is ruining my future. Please help.

A: This is deep. More than likely you will have to relocate and start a fresh new life somewhere else. People will be people, they will talk gossip, but you need someone in your life that will love you for you. Good luck. Also I hope the people reading this picked up on the source of the problem. We have to be careful about the things we say to our kids.

Q: How do you tell someone in a nice way that their dick, sex and whole bedroom scene is whack?

A: Let them know they need some work. Explain to them the whole object of sex is to be satisfied when you are done. Be honest and try not to be hurtful. This is a very touchy topic, so be gentle.

Q: I want to be married for my own reasons but I don't want kids. I want companionship, I want someone to love, I want someone to grow old with, but the thought of children does not excite me. I have lost out on many really nice guys because of the way I feel about kids. I have even thought about not telling them and just saying I can't have kids so that it's not expected of me. Adoption is not an option so I just think it's best to be honest. It seems like men down south want families and look at me strange when I say how I really feel. Please help me should. I lie or just be honest?

A: Honesty is always best. There is someone out there who does not want kids as well. You just have to wait on Mr. Right. If you lie it will come out sooner or later.

Q: I feel like the passion has died in my marriage. I want to feel that my husband wants me. Our marriage has fallen into a day-to-day routine, lacking excitement and passion. I want to break free from this. I want to know that he cares. We don't argue or fight. We just go our separate ways when we are at home. I watch TV and he plays the game in the living room. Sex is boring; I just keep asking myself what are we doing?

A: Someone has to break the cycle. It sounds like y'all need a date night and some hot steamy sex. You plan an evening out for the both of you. And the next week let him plan an evening. Plan something fun, there is this new place on Sherwood called Quarters go check it out. Hang out have fun, have sex in the car. Be creative.

Q: I met this guy recently, he is very sexy, he has a job, no kids, he is the total package. We tried to hook up but his breath is horrible. I would like to take this to the next level but I don't know what to do about this bad breath.

A: The worst-case scenario is that he might be genetically predisposed to halitosis, constant bad breath caused by an excessive amount of plaque that adheres to the whole mouth, which can be fixed by a series of deep-cleaning treatments by a dentist. Before he goes to those lengths, first suggest he brush and floss a little bit longer to tackle the plaque. And he should avoid alcohol-based mouthwashes, which can dry out the mouth and cause it to smell even worse.

Q: What if u have a man that lives with u every night and he only have sex with you once a week, twice if u lucky. And he doesn't kiss you or try to even play with you to get u on the mood? He jump straight into having sex and when u try to rub on him or play with him throughout the day he moves your hand. He tells you it irritates him or he's just not in the mood. Is it me that he is not turned on to?

A: The thrill is gone. This relationship is lacking passion. When the kissing stops this is a sign that your relationship is in trouble. Kissing between you and your spouse is a sign of affection and love for each other. I would assume that you and your partner are experiencing communication problems as well. The lack of intimacy is a sign of more serious problems. You need to address the problems that are causing you and your partner to become distant to each other. It's very difficult to be intimate with your spouse if there are other issues that need to be addressed. Just know in a relationship that has problems it is often much harder to kiss your partner and be affectionate than it is to have sex with them. Also you never said this was your husband. Find someone who is into you just as much as you are into them.

Q: My man is great as far as being a provider!!! When it comes to the bedroom he's not too passionate. I'm kind of on the wild side and I really don't know how to show that to him. He's by the book and I'm not. He almost expects me to lay on my back and that's it. That drives me nuts!!! What should I do???? Tell him or just mold him sexually? I haven't experienced anything like this before. I need advice!!!

A: You can start by communicating with him. Let him know it doesn't make him less than a man to try different positions. Get some sex games and y'all just have fun and enjoy. Let him know sex is supposed to be enjoyable for both people.

Q: If a woman is always too tired to have sex with her man when he ask her because she claim she's always tired. Is he being inconsiderate if he asks her to give him head or stroke his dick for him?

A: If a woman is always tired she needs to go see a doctor, her iron may be low etc. Personally I feel like if a man can get that dick up then it's your job to get that dick back down. What's going to happen is he's going to stop asking her about sex then she will feel played. She's going to really be hurt if she finds out he fucking someone else. We are sexual beings so as a human he should want his dick stroked and sucked and she should want the same. Another thing is sometimes as ladies we take on to much responsibility you have to assign task to everyone in your household and stop trying to do everything. I had to learn that myself.

Q: My husband and I are not living together, he lives with his mother and I live on my own, long story. Anyway I am now 54 years old and he doesn't perform the way he used to. He stays away so long from me, working and just says he's too tired to do anything, that when he comes around me I actually don't know how to please him anymore. I talk about sex with him over the phone and he says things to me, but it's not like it used to be. He's 53 and he is always calling me old but I don't act like some 54 year olds act. I love sex and I like trying new things, but he would always tell me that we are too old for that, and I get so tired of defending myself or my age. I am very active and I need to know what can I do to get him to try new things with me like sex toys, when I mention it he calls me a freak. I even had to tell him he might need help with his little friend so we went to the doctor and he gave him the pills, and we tried it once and he didn't want to do that anymore. He told me that he doesn't have a problem, yet we don't have sex two or three times a week, it's more like every three or four months. What can I do to bring that part of our relation back?

A: You are going to have to be very blunt with him and tell him "this old pussy needs to be tamed" nothing gets old but clothes. At your age having sex has so many benefits. This is what the problem is, he can't perform like he used to and he is having a hard time accepting that. Men have egos and to know that it's not working is embarrassing to him. He doesn't have to take a pill. In fact he can use a cream that does the same thing but first he has to be open. The next thing you have to do is learn to please yourself. There are some great stimulators on the market. You can't wait on the next person to make you sexually satisfied. When he ones over set the mood light some candles, play some soft music, wear some lingerie, and kiss him all over. Tell him to relax and enjoy.

Q: I'm a married man who can't get any attention from his wife. They say a closed mouth won't get fed, so I have tried talking to her, sent signs and texts, magazine clippings and all. I still don't get any attention. It is as if her mind is on someone else. I'm trying to be patient and I don't want to step out of my marriage but what else can a brother do? I love my wife dearly.

A: I have been in your wife's shoes before. When I first got married and the kids came I was so focused on being a good mother, a good home maker, cooking, cleaning, making sure everything was taken care of but I was not spending quality time with my husband. What needs to happen is you need to plan time for the two of you to be alone together so that you can get that one on one attention you are looking for. Sometimes men sit back and wait on the woman and she feels like you don't have a "serious" problem. What ladies have to realize is when your dating all of your attention is focused on one another. Once "real life" kicks in you have to keep up what you started. Plan a date night once a week. Let that be your responsibility. Once a week you go on a date. They always don't have to cost money. It could be a nice walk in the park, listening to a live band, movies, dinner, wine and painting, etc. Those are just a few ideas. Good Luck (stepping out is never the answer and your marriage will never be the same).

Q: My husband has a very low sex drive. He always said "sex isn't the most important thing" and I agreed at the time, but after three and a half years, I'm unhappy, and frustrated about the lack of sex and when I get it, its bad sex.

A: We don't get married for just sex but we do feel it's a part of the deal when we say "I do". I would never tell you to leave your husband. But I do feel you should be sexually satisfied. You have planned to spend the rest of your life with this person. You have to take matters in your own hand and invest in a vibrator, and let him know about it. Explain to him your concerns.

HONESTY AND COMMUNICATION FROM A MALE'S PERSPECTIVE:

Honesty and communication are the most important things to have in the bedroom. There is only one problem with this, men are not honest and they don't communicate in the bedroom. Part of having an amazing sex life is honesty and in order to be honest you have to communicate with your partner. As men we have to tell our partners what we enjoy and during sex. There needs to be a conversation about what sex with you will be like. And the conversation should consist of more than "I'm going to fuck your brains out "or "Girl imma beat that pussy up". Don't be afraid to get to know the sexual side of the person you're about to have sex with. You can make it fun by making it part of foreplay or talking it over during dinner but the most important thing to do is make it part of the experience.

We have to be completely honest because one small thing done in the bedroom can turn a man or woman for that matter completely off and kill the mood. You should be comfortable enough with the person you're about to share your body with enough to tell them what you enjoy. Otherwise you're just putting a gun to your dick and pulling the trigger hoping it's not loaded. You may dodge the bullet but you know you shouldn't have put yourself in that position in the first place. We have to learn to treat our bodies with more respect. Men think quantity instead of quality. They think the more women I have sex with the better my sex life will be when actually it's the opposite, because to give yourself completely to one woman in a sexual relationship with honestly and openness creates a comfortable environment to explore every sexual desire you have and to find new ones to explore. While having sex with random women can lead to ill feelings, a bad name, diseases, and all other types of fuckery. Being honest and communicating with that special person in their life can turn the bedroom into a new avenue to make your relationship stronger as a whole. Acceptance and sexual freedom with the person you love and care about is the goal before any clothing even comes off. Honesty and communication are the keys you need to open that door to sexual bliss with your partner.

CHAPTER 3

Sexual Satisfaction

Nobody wants to be in a sexual relationship with a person who is horrible in bed. Being sexually satisfied is extremely important. If you are not sexually satisfied it opens doors for all types of other problems that can be detrimental to the relationship.

Oral Sex is such a touchy topic. In most bedrooms it's a two way street, or at least it's supposed to be a two way street. We run into the woman that wants oral but doesn't want to give it or the man that gets it but very rarely goes down on his woman. Performing oral can be so much fun if you love it. In order to be good at oral sex you have to feel like you are the best at it. If you are only doing it to please your partner but you really don't enjoy it your partner will know. If oral sex is an issue for you or your partner it has to be addressed. Your partner deserves to know why you don't like oral sex.

ORAL SEX FROM A WOMAN'S POINT OF VIEW

Performing oral can be one of the most wonderful things you can do for a woman. It makes her feel loved, admired, sexy, and has the potential to give her an exceptional Orgasm. Many women prefer it to intercourse, and for those who require a large amount of clitoral stimulation, it is the easiest way to orgasm. Besides, lots of women expect it these days and men who have an excellent mouth piece are always appreciated. A woman likes to know that her partner finds her delicious; meaning that you enjoy the taste, smell and feeling of her vaginal juices. Oral sex is not exciting to a woman when she feels like a man is just doing it just to do it.

ORAL SEX FROM A MAN'S POINT OF VIEW

Most men love oral sex. It's one of the most intimate things a woman can do in the bedroom. Not only does it feel good but there is a mental factor to it also. The fact that your partner is willing to give you that type of sexual stimulation is a turn on in itself.

IMPORTANCE OF FOREPLAY FOR A WOMAN

Sex is pointless if you are not having orgasms. The reason most women are not having orgasms is because they are not being fully stimulated. It takes a woman's body about ten minutes to get fully aroused. Most men are not spending enough time on foreplay to get her in the mood. Slow down and take your time with her body. Men are rushing and not taking their time. Sex is about pleasing each other and it's not fair for you to get pleased and you're leaving your woman hanging.

QUESTIONS AND ANSWERS

Q: My dude and I like to have sex all the time. If we didn't agree on nothing else, we agreed on fucking but lately I been bored in the bedroom. Since I've been going to the strip shows and fun party it made me want to go home and spice up the bedroom. I tried new places, positions, tricks and I was giving him some fire head. Now I never was a big fan of just plain old sucking dick but to spice things up I was doing it because I knew he liked it and it turned me on knowing that I was pleasing my man. We fucked five days straight, on the sixth day he started complaining and asking me "Who turned you out" and " who you been fucking with". I thought I was doing something for both of us. Did I do something wrong?

A: You didn't do anything wrong. He's just being insecure. There is nothing worse than a man that's unsure of himself. Men I hope you're reading this, females like the bedroom to be interesting too. If she takes the time out to spice up the bedroom the last thing we want to happen is for you to start being insecure.

Q. I'm a 19 year old girl and my boyfriend is 23. We've been together for some time now but our sex has just gone downhill and now I'm bored. Our typical sex is: I'll give him oral sex, and then he always wants me to be on top during sex for the entire time. It's gotten so repetitive that I don't have orgasms anymore. I'm always the one giving and never receiving. My question is: what can I do to make sex fun for me again?

A. There are a few things that you can do before having to address this situation with your sexual partner. First, examine your role in this sexual relationship. Do you create opportunities for spontaneous sex or do you usually follow his lead? If he's as dull as you describe him to be, and you're waiting for him to spark things up, you're on the road to nowhere. Variety is the spice, and being spontaneous is what makes sex so exciting. Be spontaneous by changing up the time, location, order, speed, and intensity of your desire. Take the lead by positioning yourself into different Sexual Positions and inviting him to partake. Ask for some oral, or better yet, arrange yourself squarely on his face if he doesn't get the hint. You may want to try a sex game or fantasize out loud. You're newly found energy and enthusiasm will hopefully bring him out from hibernation and inspire him to put it down. If you have exhausted all of these options and nothing has changed, you may have a lazy lover on your hands. The only way to get through to your less active partner is by communicating how his lack of participation makes you feel. Give him the chance to explain himself and then TELL HIM WHAT YOU NEED. He'll never be able to meet your desires if he doesn't know what they are. You're future with him will be way clearer once you see how he responds to your concern. If even that doesn't work you have to ask yourself, 'Is he the one for me?'

Q: Hi first I would like to say I adore you!! I look up to you!! Anyway I'm going through a difficult situation I been with my boyfriend for eight years, we been going through so many problems and I lost attraction to him physical and mental I no longer want to have sex with him, when we're having sex I'm ready for it to be over. This has been for over two years now but he is a good provider he takes really good care of me. Okay now my first love was in jail for the last eight years he just got out and now that he is out old feelings is coming back but he have a girlfriend already it's my fault because I left him for the previous guy stated now I can't sleep nor eat because I want my first love, child father back in my life. What shall I do????

A: Please don't let your emotions lead you. Think this thing through. Your first love has been locked up for eight years he has to get himself together. He is already in a relationship, you are asking for trouble. Now the man you are with you are no longer attracted to, you have to be fair to him as well. He deserves to know the truth, why are you no longer attracted to him? Do you know why? You said so yourself that he takes really good care of you. Be wise don't act in hast.

Q: Let me start by saying I love your post. Keep them coming I'm learning a lot. Ok, My husband used to be very romantic, think only about me, but that changed a few years ago. He had an affair and I noticed that sexually he had changed. He wanted to use sex toys, put me in positions I didn't feel comfortable with. He wanted to watch adult movies while we made love. It was gross. He wasn't paying attention to ME. We weren't making love anymore. It was like we were just fucking. He wants me to take naked pictures. I feel like this woman has turned my husband out and sexually we are not on the same level. He is no longer seeing her but he tells me he needs me to be more open and step it up. I love him and I want to be everything he needs but some things I am just not comfortable with.

A: I'm glad you enjoy the post and you are learning. There is hope for your sex life because you are willing to try. This is what you do. Make a list of the things that you are not comfortable with. You and your husband go through the list and you compromise. For example you said he likes to watch porn while having sex which makes you feel gross. Purchase some soft porn with a plot. They are like real movies but the sex scenes are more graphic. That way you both are getting what you want. You have to trust your husband and know that he is not trying or going to hurt you. You have to know that what goes on in your bedroom is between the both of you. Instead of taking naked pictures purchase you some lingerie and y'all can do some role playing. You can be the model and he can be the camera man. Once you start to get comfortable, start taking little pieces off at a time. Both of you are still getting what you want. Just keep in mind sex should be fun and both people need to be satisfied in the end. Good Luck.

Q: My wife is really into getting oral sex, but I've never been into giving it. While it's not an important part of our relationship, my not performing has caused a few awkward moments, mainly because she feels like she's missing out and I feel guilty turning her down. I love her and I really want to give her what she wants, but is there anything I can do to learn to like it more?

A: You have to know why you don't like it. Is it hairy; is it ugly, does it smell, etc. what's your issue with eating pussy? I can give you a few pointers but this is something you have to want to do. The more you do it the better you will get. Keep in mind this is your wife so you should want to please her. First, slowly start kissing and fondling her as you work your way down. Once your head is between her legs, softly kiss her inner thighs. As you kiss your way down one thigh stop when you reach her pussy and give it a soft kiss (just a peck not a French kiss) continue up her other thigh. Repeat several times. Next you will do a technique I call the Suck and Swirl. First lick her from the bottom of her slit to the top. This will open her lips. Next after the lips are separated place your mouth around her clit (mouth will be medium wide open). Start to apply suction to her clit. By suction I mean a constant suction not like you would when suck on a tit. Once you have applied suction start to slowly swirl your tongue around her clit. (Now every woman is different so if she don't like her clit sucked then don't do this part) Don't just use the tip of your tongue use as much as you can. The first few seconds she will be real sensitive, when that subsides, start swirling your tongue faster. She will cum. If you really want to fuck her head up flip her over and start licking that ass too. Ohhhhhhhhh am I taking you too fast. Lol!

Q: What does that mean when a chick u messing with doesn't want to have sex and when u do it's like 1 time a week or sometimes weeks. I'm trying to spice the relationship up by doing kinky shit and the foreplay and role playing. I want to know what can I do to make her want to have sex before I cheat on her ass?

A: Cheating is never the answer it only makes things worse. If you love her then you need to see what the problem is. Sex is mental for women we have to be in a good place mentally for us to want to have sex. Meaning stress free, drama free, bills paid, kids ok, etc. Then sometimes they are just tired of your ass and just going through the motions because they don't know how to end a relationship that's not working.

Q: Why do men expect you to suck their dick but they don't like to eat pussy.

A: Because they got the game fucked up. You have to give to get. It should be like that from the beginning.

Q: I don't like when a chick ride me, I haven't found one that can make me nut. I feel like they don't know what the fuck they doing. Why they can't make me nut?

A: Because they don't know what the fuck they are doing, but they gone learn today. Ladies there is nothing worse than a lazy person in the bedroom. What y'all need a five hour energy drink? Get off your knees and get on your feet and bounce on that dick. If you got to be on your knees then you need to make the bedrock.

Q: How do I become more active during sex? It's almost like I am shy. Sometimes I try to act a fool with that DICK. I guess I'm saying give me some tips on what to do during sex some exclusive SHIT!!!

A: First of all you can't be lazy, whatever you do, don't get on your back. While he in it fuck him back, ride him like a cowboy. Don't use the bed or the bedroom. Make him talk shit to u, pull out them toys, and use your mouth. Start from his ankles and work your way up.

Q: So I've read a lot of your questions. From reading your posts, I think I am addicted to sex. Like I love sex and always seem to want it. But whenever I get it I never feel satisfied. I have never ever had an orgasm alone or with a partner. I get to point where I feel like maybe today but then nothing. Also something that concerns me is that I have a hard time saying no. I always feel compelled even when I don't want to (which isn't often). Like if my partner is asking I will just to satisfy him. Another thing is I am EXTREMELY quiet during sex. I guess I kind of feel stupid making sounds. My partner sometimes doesn't think I am having a good time because of my lack of noise but I am I just can't for some reason verbalize it. IDK. What can I do about this? I mean I want to have enjoyable sex. I want to achieve an orgasm. And I want to be able to let him know that he is working it right. Any advice?

A: Glad you're reading the post. First sex should be agreed upon by both people. The whole point of having sex is to have an orgasm. You need to learn to masturbate. You have to get to know your own body. Start off with a bullet and some arousal cream. Once you get it down, teach your man how to please you. There is no way you are having sex as much as you say and he's letting you get up unsatisfied. Making noise is natural during sex. This lets your partner know they are pleasing you. If he is making you feel good you need to let him know. This will only make him want to please you more. First you have to work on getting that orgasm.

Q: What's up? First let me thank you for everything you are doing to help educate people about sex. I have a question but it's for a friend of mine. She is dating this guy that doesn't like to receive head and doesn't like her to ride him. She thinks this is very weird and so do I. I couldn't give her an answer that could possible make sense so I thought maybe you could help me with this one.

A: One thing that I have learned is that every man is different and want it takes to please one my not please another. I don't know what type of personality he has but he sounds "old fashion" to me. It sounds like he wants to be in control at all times. Some men know that when they lay on their back it slows up the blood circulation and they start to go soft. That might be his problem. As far as giving head. I have met a few men that feel like its degrading to women and only whores do it. Everyman is different is all I can say. But he sounds kind of boring in the bedroom she might want to get him some flicks. Lol!

SEXUAL ISSUES IN A SEXUAL RELATIONSHIP

Most people that have a sexual issue are too ashamed to talk about their "little problem" and I say it like that because most problems can be fixed. Some of the most common problems with women is they are not being stimulated properly to get an orgasm, so they just have sex and never get anything out of it but are scared to tell the man they are with they are not getting anything out of the whole sexual experience. One of the most common problems in men is erectile dysfunction. The dick isn't getting hard because the blood isn't circulating to it properly.

Men please listen to your woman if she tells you it's time to step it up in the bedroom. Making love to a woman does not mean putting your dick in and humping. Making love means taking your time and exploring her body from head to toe. Touching every hot spot, stroking her hair will send chills though her body, kissing her neck, stomach, in between her thighs, licking that pussy right and licking that ass. I'm talking about taking her body to another level. Handle Your Business MEN!

Q: Hello Mrs. Parker, I love giving oral but I need someone who will give it back. Can you help me out please?

A: When you are dating someone and you think this could possibly be a sexual relationship then certain questions need to be asked. Ask the other person how do they feel about oral sex?? If she says she don't care for it then you know it's going to be a one sided relationship, on the other hand if she tells you she loves it then you know she is a keeper. Lol

Q: I really need your help and want an answer from you and your husband. I am having a dilemma with sucking my man's dick. I like to suck dick I feel like I'm good at what I do but I don't get in the habit of sucking everybody's dick except my man's. We have been together since 2005 on and off and now we have been permanent with our relationship since 2008. We are now engaged to one another. I must admit, I feel a little guilty because my man pleases me more orally than I do him. I don't even have to ask. I get licked from the roota-to-da-toota but I may suck his dick like once a month. He never complains and he knows my reason why: he is not circumcised. I don't know what it is about it but just thinking of me doing it disgusts me. I don't want to seem like that person who is free to receive but not give and I don't want to be selfish, I just hate doing it. I have told him that I think he needs to do it, not just for me to suck his dick but in order for him to be clean and healthy down there. He feels at his age (over 30) it does not make sense to get it done. But if he expect me to suck that dick on da regular I think he needs to get it done. What can I do to get beyond this?

A: This is what you can do: get some flavored condoms and play a game with him. Every time you want to suck his dick give him a flavored condom during a moment that is not sexual. That way you put it on his mind all day. He will know that he is getting his dick sucked that night. Good Luck!

Q: I'm with a man that cannot eat coochie. When my boyfriend goes down on me, I don't really feel anything. I often fake it when he does. I know it's him because other men that I have been with had me climbing the walls. Is there anything I can do?

A: You can start by teaching him. Guide him let him know when it feels good to you. Teach him to open your vaginal lips so that your clit can be exposed. The other thing you can do is watch some porn so he can see an example of what he needs to do.

Q. My boyfriend and I want to have oral sex, but the problem is that I have braces on the front and the back of my teeth. He insists that it's okay and that he will be fine, but I'm worried that I will cut him. What's the best thing to do?

A: If this is something that both you and your partner want to go ahead with, it means tweaking your technique. If you think a little extra protection might be needed you can try using dental wax, dental silicone or even a silicone or plastic mouth guard. Your dentist or orthodontist can determine the mouth guard that will provide the best protection for your unique mouth work (just tell them it's for sports if you feel a little shy to let on to the real reason). If you are using a condom for oral sex, I would recommend changing it before switching to vaginal or anal sex.

Q: I don't mind going down, but my girl doesn't shave. She says it makes her itch.

A: Ladies you got to get that "jungle love" under control. Shave that shit. Nobody likes eating bush cookies anymore. There is this shaving cream called Coochy, it's a rash free shaving cream. I promise you're going to feel so much better and cleaner when you get rid of that shit.

Q: Why don't more men lick your ass during sex, men act like they scared to do it?

A: Unfortunately all men aren't freaks like that. You also have to be vocal about what you like. They can't read your mind.

Q: If you were fucking a man and he just came out the blue and asked you to lick his ass, how would you feel? What would you say and would you think different about that man?

A: I would think he has had it before. What would I say? Shit, I thought I knew you better than that. Would I think differently? He would no longer be my man, boo, baby, whatever.

Q: Is it a good thing to eat married woman or single woman's pussy?

A: OK if you want to eat a married woman's pussy you must want to taste her husband's dick in your mouth. If you want to eat a single woman's pussy you must want to taste a lot of dicks in your mouth. How about you find your own pussy. Make sure it's clean and disease free and eat that one.

Q: I don't mind giving oral sex but I do mind the position I'm in when I'm giving it. My boyfriend likes me to get on my knees and I feel it's so demeaning. He wants me to look up at him. He treats me like I'm doing porn.

A: Look at this way: you are your man's personal porn star. Don't over think it. Do a little role playing. Let yourself go. Men are visual they like to see you do real nasty things to them. If it makes you feel better sit in a chair and have him stand in front of you.

Q: My boyfriend doesn't like getting head cause of what happened in his past, and I'm running out of ideas can u give a sisters some new ideas were a wild n freaky couple so any and everything goes.

A: What happened in his past?

Response: He got bit

A: Oh shit!!!!!

Response: Left a scar

A: Wow!!!! I am speechless. I know this had to leave some type of psychological impact on him. I probably wouldn't want head ever again. He has to trust that you would never do anything like this to hurt him. If you are looking to do something different try some role playing, wear sexy lingerie, lap dances, and sex in public places. Oral sex can be such a major factor and to eliminate it completely put so many limits on your sex life.

Q: I know that sucking dick is all a part of grown sex. My question is what do you recommend when sucking dick that will make your man nut in less than five minutes.

A: I can't promise you he will nut in five minutes but I will tell this - he will enjoy it. When you are sucking dick men like you to get real sloppy. Just lose yourself for a moment take that dick and slap yourself in the face with it, lick and suck his balls, and spit on it. Just get real nasty. The nastier you get the harder his dick will get. You should deep throat it every now and then. Use some oral sex candy and let the candy stimulate him. Every man is different and oral sex is something that shouldn't be rushed. Enjoy yourself and take your time and cater to him. He will cum when he gets ready.

Q: Hi All. Do any of you have any suggestions on what to do when you have a dry mouth and you want (or he wants it) to give your man oral sex? it seems like each time I go to do that my mouth gets dry (or is already dry), and I know that when my mouth is dry it doesn't feel that good to him. I know to give a good BJ your mouth has to be nice and moist. Any thoughts or suggestions? Thank you

A: You can drink water right before, you can use a flavored body topping or you can use Good Head Sucker to activate the saliva hands in your mouth.

Q: When a man nut while eating pussy is that saying he is turned on?

A: These are called "No touch orgasms" technically, "wet dreams" would fall under this category. In order for a man to ejaculate it requires some form of stimulation. Even if it's not physical stimulation it can be mental stimulation. In young males it is not uncommon for a boy to ejaculate during heavy petting. Orgasms actually occur in the brain, and the combination of anticipation, seeing a woman's body, and touching may cause an orgasm without touching his dick.

Q: I feel so horrible for my husband when I'm having a period. You're tired, moody, cramping, and irritable and not feeling sexy at the moment (maybe it's just me) what are some other things you can do to please your man and still keep him satisfied when it's that time of the month??

A: You can suck his dick or you can use a pocket pussy it's a masturbator for a man.

Q: I requested you because I have a question. I have been seeing this guy for several months now. His sex is okay but he's a cute, fine, sexy hard worker and I just love his personality. We have a good connection but the sex is alright. I never gets to have an organism and he be trying to make me have one but I just can't. His not big down there from what I'm used to. What advice can you give me to make our sex better and for me to have orgasm?

A: Sometimes using direct stimulation with his finger or his mouth will give you that orgasm. Brining in a toy won't hurt. There is a toy called a Fat Boy that he can use this will make him appear to be larger.

Q: Hey me and my girlfriend been together for two years n I love sex I like hips ass n thighs I give her head lick her ass I do it all ill have sex three times a day if she let me BUT she ONLY nuts (orgasms) when she on top but I love hitting it doggy style. What are other ways or tips?

A: The reason she is ONLY cumming (having an orgasm) when she is on top is because she is applying direct stimulation to her clit. There are different types of orgasms but it sounds like se is only getting clitoral orgasms. You can put her in different positions but you still need to use your fingers and play with her clit while you are in the position. Another thing you can try is some Vibrating Lovers Thongs. She can wear them while she is in any position and her clit will be stimulated the whole time.

Q: Is it normal to have multiple orgasms? Like over 20 every time I have sex and I get dehydrated afterwards and even lose weight. Weird

A: Well aren't you the lucky lady. That's a good thing. I'm taking it that you are a squitter like me. Yes you feel drained that is normal. Just get him to get you some water afterwards you will be alright. As far as the weight loss, you burn so many calories having sex and if you are not replacing what you have burned with some food you can expect to lose weight.

Q: Ok I finally got this squirting thing down but is it normal for your body to hurt after???

A: When you have this type of orgasm your muscles will contract and spasm and twitch for a while (30-60 seconds after wards) and you will have jelly legs and sometimes you are using muscles that you haven't used in a while.

Q: After I have an orgasm (a really big one) I get a headache. Why is this?

A: It's due to the swift rise in blood pressure that occurs during sex and, more particularly, during orgasm. Sometimes, orgasm headaches occur when a person is under intense emotional stress as well.

Q: Why do some men have two orgasms at one time?

A: If you are counting muscle contractions, then yes men can have multiple orgasms. They can cum and their penis never goes down. They are able to continue have sex.

Q: What Are the Causes of a Loose Vagina?

A: One of the most common causes of vaginal loosening is due to birth giving. The more a woman gives birth, the higher is the propensity for her vagina to slacken because her vaginal walls are stretched out. Another cause of loosening of the vagina is due to frequent sexual activity. Men prefer tight vagina, having a tight vagina will intensify his feeling of arousal and would make her feel every thrust and pressure done by him.

Q: Would putting powdered sugar in a vagina cause any kind of irritation?

A: Because vaginas are dark, warm, and moist, and penises are not. The vaginal environment is much more welcoming to yeast and bacteria which also happen to like sugar. Thus, if you put sugar on your vagina, you'll be more likely to get an infection.

Q: I want to try Ben Wa Balls but I want them to arouse me do you have any suggestions?

A: Rocking with the balls inside the vagina will stimulate you. Get into a sitting position and rock back and forth with your legs pressed together. If you want to do a little grind, that will help. The other thing you can do is try the vibrating Ben Wa Balls. They are small on a cord and they will vibrate and stimulate the g-spot.

Q. Before I met my boyfriend, my friend had convinced me to buy a vibrator from you Mrs. Parker, a very wise buy I might add! I told my boyfriend about it early in our relationship and he used it on me. It was awesome. We had started having sex by then and I hate to say it, but my vibrator has been doing a better job than my boyfriend has. He came to your store and got me a bigger and better one for my birthday and I would rather use that than him! I want him to be able to have longer stamina and be able to perform sex much better. How do I tell him this without hurting his ego?

A. Sex toys can be great fun within a relationship but they should be an enhancement, not a replacement, to your sex life. It is possible that you have become so focused on your toy play that you are not giving enough focus to what you can personally do to improve sex with your boyfriend. You imply that you have just started having sex with him. If this is his first experience of sex it may be a mixture of nerves, inexperience, and lack of knowledge that is causing the problems. The solution requires some effort from him to educate himself and some patience and encouragement on your part to help him do so.

Q: Why do friends feel like you not supposed to fuck someone they have fucked? Y'all are not married. Then they say you want their leftovers, everybody know that leftovers are better.

A: I was taught that fucking people your family or friends have fucked is off limits. You are right they are not married, but it's all about your values and what you think is important to you. Be prepared to ruin friendships and to not be trusted by anyone.

Q: Hi there wanted to ask what I can do I been with husband almost twenty years I got sick years ago and became very obese to where we couldn't have sex but doggy style which I do love but he cums to quick I recently had surgery and weight is coming off good plus my cycle has been problems for years I also had that taken care of in two weeks I can have sex again I want to spice things up but he not into trying kinky stuff so what can I do for pleasure since he despises toys and massagers. I personally feel he is threatened but I need to be satisfied what might I do.

A: Ask him how he would feel if he was not being satisfied sexually. This is not about toys or massagers but being satisfied sexually. I don't care if he has to use his mouth, finger, or elbow when y'all finish having sex you should be satisfied. You have to be honest with your husband tell him he cums before you can even start enjoying the sex. I know you said he doesn't want to use anything but not using anything is leaving you sexually starved.

Q: *My 12 year old found my vibrator while looking for batteries in my night stand. I'm a little embarrassed but my husband just laughed it off. She thought it was a massager. Do I tell her what it really is?*

A: That's just what it is a massager, she doesn't have to know it massages the pussy. LOL. Keep it simple, she's not even thinking about that any more. Get you a hide your vibe pillow and you don't have to worry about that happening again.

Q: *Why do men feel threatened by a toy?*

A: Well they can't do what a toy can do because they were not designed to. Most men know that and they fear you will want the toy more than you want them. They need to remember a toy just gives you a quick orgasm, but it can't hold you, talk to you, etc.

Q: *I have used my bullet so much until my clit is sore. Why is this?*

A: You have your bullet turned up to high. Also you are applying to much pressure.

Q: *My boyfriend likes me to beat his meat, but I find it so boring.*

A: Jack him off with a string of pearls. Use lots of lubrication then wrap the pearls around the shaft of his dick, slowly stroking them up and down. It will drive him crazy. The next option is to buy him a Beaded Pussy. This masturbator feels like a real woman inside.

Q: Ok my man has a fat dick but it's not long. Sometimes it's like I can't really get that feeling that I'm looking for.

A: He will feel bigger and longer if you put your legs over his shoulders when having sex in the missionary position. Doing this shortens your vaginal canal, so he'll feel much longer.

Q: Whenever we have sex he just lay there like a dead fish, am I doing something wrong?

A: Try having sex standing up, get his ass up out that bed. Tell him we fucking everywhere but the damn bed. The more into it you are, the more he will get into it and might even like it. There is nothing worse than a lazy lover.

Q: If his cum looks like water what does that mean???????

A: A man's "first nut" will look thick and sticky, and may feel a bit like jelly and clump together in globs. Scientists think that semen does this so that if the man has had sex with a woman and has cum inside her the semen stays there longer and does not leak out. Between five and 40 minutes after this, his "cum" becomes more liquid and watery and contains less sperm. So what does that tell you? If he bringing home water to you he has already gotten that first nut somewhere else.

Q: Why do some men have a lot of Precum?

A: The same way a woman gets aroused and her body gets wet, a man gets aroused and his body produces Pre-cum. The more aroused he gets the more his body produces. Precum is lubricant for the body. Research shows that most precum does not contain sperm; however, it does contain viruses such as HIV if that person is infected.

Q: I am a 42 year old woman with a high sex drive. I always have a wet vagina and never had any problems in the bedroom. I recently found out that I have to have a hysterectomy. I want to know will the surgery change my sex drive and the moisture of my vagina???

A: Sexual activity after a hysterectomy has been studied extensively, and most women who have a healthy sex life return to that level of activity. Some women find that they are more interested in sex after surgery, especially those who had concerns about pregnancy or chronic pelvic pain. There are differences between the types of surgery. One study showed that women who had a hysterectomy that left the cervix in place were more likely to orgasm during sexual intercourse as the cervix plays a role in vaginal orgasms. The study also showed that the ability to have clitoral orgasms, or external orgasms, was not changed by surgery regardless of the presence of the cervix. Some patients do experience a feeling of loss or depression after surgery, and some begin menopause, decreasing sex drive. If these symptoms are handled effectively, the patient can expect to experience a full and active sex life. Some women will require a lubricant to have sex without discomfort after their hysterectomy, as the surgery can cause some vaginal dryness.

Q: I only had sex once with my first love then I got a new boo. Now I'm ready to give him the business. I'm a little nervous I don't know where to begin can you give me any pointers??

A: Sex is something that has to feel right, the place, the timing, etc. Just go with the flow, your mind and body will tell you when you are ready to give up the goods. At the end of the day you want to feel like you have made the right choice.

Q: I have a very big vagina, I've been asked by several family members and friends "Are you wearing a pad" because it's that noticeable, they tell me things like you have fat, big, coochie. This is embarrassing is this normal?

A: Most women are proud to have a fat cat (at least among African Americans), but to answer your question, you have a large pubic bone. There is nothing wrong with you. If you're overweight, you can also develop a big pad of fat that will make it look even larger. Ask any man on my page if they like a fat cat and see what they say. If you were in PPG I would tell you to post it up and let them be the judge. LOL.

Q: What are some things that a woman can do to help her get in the mood quick? I've tried alcohol which seems to work every time, but I want something different. Any suggestions?

A: 1. Try eating one ounce of dark chocolate, it increases production of serotonin. It is the body's natural feel-good chemical that leads to heightened stimulation and arousal. 2. Purchase some Cleopatra Secret or Orgasmix both are arousal creams that work really well.

Q: I recently had sex last night and we used a condom and such but like half way during the sex I realized I was starting to swell down there today I am in extreme pain and can barely walk. It hurts so bad. I have never seen anything like this. I need help. Do you have any tips that might bring down the swelling? I am in extreeeeeeeme pain. I am too embarrassed to talk about it to anybody.

A: It sounds like you have a latex allergy. Take some time and soak in some warm water. This will help with the swelling. If you feel like this didn't help then you should contact your doctor. Next time get some LAMB SKIN condoms they cost more but you won't have to worry about this happening again.

Q: What should mates do to make the woman comfortable with anal sex? What do you do to prevent the pain from the penis entering? Please give us some tips?

A: Relax and use a fleet, some anal ease and Astroglide. Please take your time, use as much lube as you like.

Q: *My mother moved in with me and my wife wants to have sex all the time. I'm not comfortable with my mother being in the next room. My wife gets so mad with me when I tell her no. Why?*

A: WTF! If I was your wife I would be pissed. Homeboy you got to grow up. You don't think your mother knows you and your wife have sex? She is in your house. You shouldn't deprive your wife. Don't get mad when she leave your ass. Remember this: happy wife, happy life.

Q: *I have a male friend that likes to eat pussy but he always get a cramp in his tongue.*

A: This is caused by lack of salts like sodium and potassium in the diet. The tongue is a muscle, so he could try eating bananas that should help.

Q: *I'm asking this question for a friend. How does she make her man nut while she sucking his dick? She feels like she is doing a good job but she just can't make him cum?*

A: Get you a tongue dinger, it's a vibrating tongue ring. Make sure you go up and down on that vein. Get sloppy when you suck that dick and spit on his shit.

Q: *What do you do if you trying to ride that dick but the man is just so wide you can barely get your legs around him?*

A: Froggy style my girl. You can try still being on top but instead of using your knees keep your feet planted. This way you'll be able to reach and control the movement. He'll like it if you do the same position with you facing the same way he is facing. That way he can watch that ass move.

Q: My boyfriend and I have been together since last May. He has two problems. Like when we have sex either he comes to quick or can't stay hard. We've tried masturbation before during and after sex and it doesn't work. Same thing with oral don't really work. Me on top doesn't really work all like that. This is a problem that is really depressing him and I don't know what to do? I love him with all my heart and soul and told him that. He keeps thinking if he doesn't please me another man will. I reassure him that I would never cheat.

A: He needs to use Stay Hard Cream and a Cock Ring. The cock ring will help him stay harder longer and the cream will get him hard. I sell both at The PPG Store.

Q: I need a woman to handle me in bed. I want her to toss me on her bed and take advantage of me. To just take that dick, rape me, do whatever she wants? Why can't I get this from a woman?

A: Women are not aggressive but if you like that kind of shit then I can hook her up with some blindfolds, handcuffs, and whips. A closed mouth won't get feed, so you better start talking.

Q: Every chick I'm with feel like she got good pussy, I feel like they should let me be the judge. What makes all women feel like they got good pussy?

A: The same reason all men feel like they know how to put the dick down. I know that shit ain't true from the shit I read in my inbox. Maybe she feels like it is good because it's tight, smell good or disease free. Who am I to judge I ain't never fucked no woman.

Q: I am 46 and I like a juvie ...these old men really don't know how to knock the pussy out, why is that? The juvie know how to put it down like I like it but the old men has all the money.

A: I'm pretty sure when those old men were young they could put it down too, but as time goes on our bodies change. The young boys got energy because most of them don't work and they have nothing but time on their hands, the old men be tired cause they have worked all day to get that money you like. The juvie doesn't have anything to offer but his dick, so you have to think about what's important to you. Get your old man a pump.

Q: My man doesn't like to go down. He says he don't like the way I taste. He say I'm "tart". It hurts my feelings. I love going down on him not because he tastes like chocolate or anything but because I love pleasing him. I feel like it's unfair.

A: You got to give to receive. You got two choices stop sucking his dick, or get you some Yummy Cummy. I don't know what pussy taste like but I know that shit that come out of them is tart as hell. Increase your fruit intake and cut back on salt.

Q: I gave it to my man every day, sometimes twice a day and he still cheated, could it be that some men are just dogs?

A: Some men are, just as well as some women are. People cheat for different reasons. Some do it just because they know they can. They know if you find out you're going to stay so they don't have anything to lose. Others do it because the relationship is lacking something like making him feel like a man, just having someone he can talk to etc.

Q: Mostly every time my husband and I have sex, I always catch a cramp right when it's getting good or after I climax. I NEED HELP!!!

A: Your body is lacking potassium, you can get some pills from GNC or you can eat a lot of bananas. Drink plenty of water. That will solve your problem.

Q: I been with my dude for two years now and we have a great sex life. I never tell him no and never has to ask more than once for sex. Ok so here my issue, he wants to have anal sex and we have tried but it is the most painful feeling in the world to me and he can't get it in. We have tried anal ease, ice, lubricants and none that does work. I always aim to please my man because he's so good to me but I need some help/advice on how to get that monster in there before he is no longer satisfied with me sexually???

A: Let me start off by saying I'm glad to hear you are doing whatever it takes to please your man. It sounds like he is a very large man. Lol. But it can be done. You need an anal training kit. These are butt plugs that are different sizes. What you do is train your anus to open up. The kit comes with three sizes once you can wear the large one with comfort then your man will be able to fit with no problem. You also need a lube shooter. This shoots the anal ease all the way in the anal area without any wasting out. That way you are comfortable through the whole process. I hope this helps. Just for the record butt plugs feel really good especially when they vibrate.

Q: What you call it if a woman asks her man for sex and he's always giving her excuses not to have sex? What should she do? Does that mean he is getting it from somewhere else?

A: Most men don't turn a woman down for sex. Either his dick broke or he fucking somebody else. Men if I'm wrong please correct me.

Q: When I suck my husband off I continue sucking (gently) long after he's finished and begins to soften. This accomplishes two things; he gets sucked dry (something he loves) and it gives my mouth time to make sufficient saliva to dilute his semen which I let pool near the front of my mouth and under my tongue. When I really have a mouth full he likes me to gargle his cum but it taste so nasty. Give me some tips.

A: Yummy Cummy is a blend of core fruit extracts and concentrates with the addition of both parley and celery in substantial quantities to act as an odor and taste neutralizer, it makes his cum taste sweet.

Q: I have anal ease, do I need lubricant as well?

A: Anal Ease is used for numbing that area not lubricating that area. You will still need some type of lubricant. Water based lubes always work well, but you can also use anal lubes. Anal lubes are simply a thicker gel rather than a liquid. This thicker consistency is preferable because it helps the lubricant stay in place. Some lubricants contain benzocaine, an anesthetic which will help numb you as well.

Q: Before I had my baby I NEVER "ran" from the dick, but after baby I now find myself "running" why is that?

A: Of course the birth of a baby does a number on your body. After you have your baby you should do lots of Kegals. What happens is your vaginal area has widen which means you are taking in more dick than you did before. That's where the pain is coming from. Just tell him to take it easy.

Q: For some reason my child's father and I have this love/hate relationship. We both have other people in our lives but we still find time to fuck each other. After sex we are back beefing until we fuck again. I keep telling myself I'm not going to do it anymore and he does the same thing but we always end up talking to each other, falling out with each other, and of course back fucking each other. What is wrong with me?

A: It sounds like you both have a really good sexual connection and you all might even love each other but when it comes to real life and responsibility y'all clash. I just really feel bad for the people in your life. The bad part is more than likely the two of y'all will end up back together and the other people will get hurt in the process. Y'all are just attracted to each sexually.

Q: Why is it always the men who ain't shit that have the best dick? No job, car, house, but he got some good dick.

A: This is my opinion, those men could make something of themselves but the women that they run into make them feel as long as they putting the dick down they don't have to do nothing else. My mama always told me I could get a wet ass by myself. So big dick or no dick at all you got to have something more to offer me than just that.

Q: Hey my man is in jail and I was wondering what I could get to satisfy me until he returns.

A: You have three options: You can get a Wall Banger if you like deep penetration. You place the Wall Banger up against the wall and you back up to it and fuck yourself. They come in many different sizes and they feel real with veins and all. Next there is a Flicker, this toy is a stimulator. It's used for direct stimulation to the clit. It feels like someone is moving their tongue fast on your clit. Last there is a toy called a Jack Rabbit. This is a combination toy. It has a shaft and a clit stimulator. The shaft rotates in the pussy stimulating the G-Spot and the bunny ears stimulate the clit at the same time. I don't know how long he is going to be gone but just know that you can please yourself just as good if not better than any man can.

Q: I have a situation and don't know how to approach it. I've been with my son's father for almost five years now. He's not well endowed like I would prefer. But in the beginning sex was okay, it was never really great and I always have to make myself cum. It's gotten to the point where I make up excuses so that he won't even touch me, and when I do give in its obvious I'm not enjoying it but he doesn't that. It feels disgusting and I just want him to get off of me and leave me alone. I felt that I have tried options to make it better but I get the same results. Help me please. You can share this if you would like, I would like others' feedback as well.

A: There are a few things you can do. First you have to have that talk with him and let him know you love him but he does not satisfy you in the bedroom. This WILL hurt his feelings because he is a man. Let him know you would never think of leaving him you just need him to be open to some new ideas. Option 1: You can purchase him a penis extension. This will extend his length two to four inches. Option 2: You can purchase a cock ring this will swell the shaft and make it appear to be bigger. Option 3: You can purchase a pump and this will stretch him out over time. Option 4: You can purchase a dildo the size that you like and after he has cum you can let him fuck you with the dildo and perform oral on you at the same time.

Q: Why does the penis have a hook?

A: Sometimes blood fills the caverns unevenly. For example if there's more blood on the left, the penis is "fuller" on the left. The penis will curve to the right.

Q: My boyfriend loses his erection every time he puts a condom on. Why is this? Does he need to use or take something that will keep his erection strong when he puts on a condom? Is it a mental thing? There is no problem with him maintaining his erection as long as there is no condom involved. Please help.

A: When a man puts on a condom it changes the feeling. Try using ultra-thin condoms, let him put a little lube in the inside before he puts it on this will give him a more natural feeling. He might want to even try a cock ring. That will help it stay up.

Q: I been with my boyfriend now for seven years. We are 11 years apart at the beginning of our relationship sex was AWESOME anytime and anyplace he was ready. Now since he found out he have diabetes he can't get it up or don't last long. It's very frustrating for us both. I'm glad we have a good relationship without it but when you want it and can't have it what do you do......

A: The medication that he is taking causes him to have poor blood circulation to the penis. Prolong Plus Cream basically make the blood circulate the way it's supposed to which causes him to have an erection. He can also use a cock ring as well if he wants it to stay up a long time.

Q: When you reach a certain age do you stop Squirting?

A: As long as you are able to get stimulated properly you will be able to squirt.

Q: I have discovered the only way I can have an orgasm is when I use a shower head. It feels so good and I have the water coming out super hard. I've never been able to have an orgasm with any of my partners. Is something wrong with me? The guy I'm in a relationship with now for about two years is very frustrated with me. I don't blame him, I know it hurts his manhood but it's not his fault. We've tried every position possible so now we are asking for your help.

A: No there is nothing wrong with you. The clit is covered by skin and sometimes it is not exposed unless you are completely aroused. Your clit needs lots of stimulation. Your man can use his finger but it will be more intense if you had a Frisky Finger. This is a stimulator that he wears on his finger. He needs to play with the pussy a little more that's it. All women do not get orgasms through penetration but most will get one through stimulation.

Q: First. Keep up the good work I love reading your post/comments. With that being said, I've been with my man for eight years. We share a son together and six months ago we just decided to move in together. We have been through a lot and cheating has been a factor on his behalf, but I chose to stay. Now, I'm to the point where I don't even care anymore. It's like I'm looking forward to the future while he's stuck in neutral. Any suggestions??

A: Boy when a woman's fed up there ain't nothing you can do about it. Y'all have a child together and I would express my feelings to him. I would set a time frame to see some growth and if I didn't see what I needed to see then I would let him know that I care about him but I need more.

Q: My boyfriend and I have been talking for several months now and I find that he can't stay aroused long. I've tried all types of things to arouse him but it just doesn't seem to work. One minute he's hard as a rock then he's back soft again! He's one of the men that likes to watch porn and jack off from time to time. I had to ask was it me or what, he says no! Does he need to stop jacking off or what!? I NEED SOME ADVICE

A: Trust me it's not you. He knows how to stimulate himself that's why he was hard while watching porn. Not to mention men are visual creatures so that freaky shit they are doing turns them on. You need to be his porn star. Get him some Prolong Plus and a Cock Ring. Talk some nasty shit, wear something slutty and get his attention.

Q: What's the best position to do with a man that over 300 lbs?

A: If you have a partner that is over 300 lbs, you should invest in a position pillow. What this does is put you in a wedge position so that your pussy is elevated. This way he does not have to lean over on top of you. Next the saying goes "If he has a gut, then let it rest on your butt. (Doggie Style). Last you can curl up in a knot and let him get behind you. You will be laying down he will be sitting up (the pillow works good for this one too).

Q. Every time my man goes deep it really hurts (Doggie Style). It gets really painful and then I'm completely put off with the idea of sex, and then I just worry about further pain. If he goes slow than it's boring; if he goes slow and deep, it begins to hurt. But if he goes faster and faster, it really hurts and in many cases I tell him to stop and I feel bad like I'm doing something wrong. He tells me he's OK about it, but I feel I'm not satisfying him. How do you reduce the pain? Are there any sex positions that could be recommended?

A. First of all, you are not doing anything wrong and your man is right to tell you that it is absolutely okay. What is not okay is that you are experiencing pain. Second of all, just because standard doggy style is not working for you doesn't mean that your sex life has to be boring or that you cannot satisfy your man. Doggy-style is a favorite position for many men, but it isn't always a comfortable for all women, especially when it is causing pain. The length of the vagina varies from woman to woman, and if the length of your man's penis is longer than your vagina, you may find that the discomfort is from him bumping up against your cervix. If you want to continue to try this position you may want to make some changes and do a little trial-and-error, while listening to your body and not doing anything that causes you pain. From the standard doggy style position on all fours, you can try a few things like squeeze your legs together, rather than having them open, and have your chest level with your bottom rather than allowing your back to arch. Reach back and put your hand on his lower abdomen, this way you can control how hard and deep he goes. Lay on your stomach and have him enter you from behind, again with your legs pressed together tight. Use lots of lubricant this will help. Good Luck.

Q: In the past 24 hours my fiancé and I have had sex twice and both times we were in the middle of sex, we switch positions and he instantly goes soft. Is this normal?

A: Sometimes a man wants to have sex but his body has other plans. It sounds like when you switch positions he is no longer being stimulated. Invest in a cock ring this will keep him hard the whole time. Only remove the ring when you are completely finished. If this keeps happening make a doctor's appointment he may be starting to experience erectile dysfunction.

Q. I am a slim man 6'1" 189lbs and my wife is 5'8" 425lbs and what I was wondering what are the best positions I can use to give my wife something very special in intercourse? Sometimes it seems like I can't get in all the way. Thanks in advance for your help.

A. Any position that keeps excess weight away from her pubic area will assist in penetration of a heavier woman. Therefore, it would be helpful to have her butt slightly elevated on a position pillow. Try her laying back at the edge of the bed with her knees drawn up and wide. Also, don't forget that you can pleasure her by performing cunnilingus. This will allow a lot of direct stimulation. You know I love to recommend a toy for stimulation as well.

Remember to experiment and see what works for the both of you. Good luck!

Q: I need your advice on this. My man picked up some pounds since he was in jail and our sex life is not the same. I've started eating healthy and lost 20lbs. How do I get him to do the same without crushing his manhood? I believe cause of the weight his dick has gotten smaller.

A: This is a fact the fatter a man is the smaller he can look because the fat at the base of a man's abdomen covers up the foundation of the shaft, making him look smaller than he actually is. So, by decreasing the amount of fat on the body you enable more of his penis to be viewed, which actively "lengthens" the penis. Losing up to 15 pounds of fat can increase the look of a penis by half an inch to two inches. A lot of men are packing but you will never be able to see their true size because of all the fat at the base.

Q: I have a question, I'm a plus size female and I have never been able to ride a man. I've had a man try to teach me and help me but I give up easy and it always seems as if I can't move my body. So question 1 is what can I do to be more comfortable in moving my body? Next I would like to practice but not with a man lol and definitely not a woman but I have toys. Is it possible to practice using toys if so what kind?

A: There are two position aids you can try. Take the strain off your thighs and enjoy weightless sex! Bounce up and down on your partner with ease, and try new positions while enjoying moves you never thought were possible!

The Fetish Fantasy Sex Stool is designed to play hard. Or you can try The Hot Seat. It's designed for those long, hard rides, the cushion's flocked material and E-Z Grip Luv Handles make the journey more enjoyable.

Q: I DO NOT KNOW HOW TO RIDE, and what makes it so difficult is that it is my boyfriend's favorite position, is there any advice on what I can do to make it work for the both of us, I like the position but I dread doing it because I am not experienced in it, and I'm not real flexible. my legs hurt after a while also and I don't know why, he is a little bigger than me so I know there spread open a little more, but is there any ideas on how to make it work better.??

A: Don't over think it. It's just riding. Try this instead of being on your knees, kind of squat on him and that should work fine. Bounce up and down. Also try one knee down one knee up. Last, you can ride him with your legs in front of you on his shoulders. Do what feels good to you. Talk to him and ask him if he likes it. Reverse cowgirl is a winner. Try that as well.

Q: So, I've been dating this guy for a couple months. I really like him. It's like we click! I can talk to him about anything and we have so much fun together. We've been discussing getting into a relationship, but I'm hesitant on doing so now. We recently became sexually active with one another and I'm not satisfied at all. Don't get me wrong, he knows how to perform in the bedroom. His penis is just not what I expected, although his tongue performance does make up for his lack. But, I feel his tongue can only do so much. I need to feel him inside of me!! I thought it would've gotten better after the first time, but it's the same. When we had sex, all I could think about is having sex with my ex because he was THE BOMB.COM!! What can I do to make the sex better because I do like him and want to see where things could possibly go between us?! I LOVE having sex so I can't see myself being with someone who can't satisfy my EVERY need!!

A: It sounds like he is not that big. If I was in this situation I would invest in a dildo. I would not get a vibrator because you're looking for a more natural feeling. You can be very creative with toys. As long as you're getting the right stimulation and penetration your body will be satisfied. Let him fuck you from behind and then fuck you with the dildo. Better yet suck his dick while fucking yourself with a wall banger. (This is a toy with a suction cup attached). This may not be the normal type of sex you're used to, but this sex will be exciting and different.

SEXUAL SATISFACTION FROM A MAN'S POINT OF VIEW:

Sexual Satisfaction has a lot to do with personal responsibility. As I stated in the other chapters it is our responsibility to express what turns us on and the things we enjoy sexually. It's like the old saying "A closed mouth don't get fed". First of all you have to know what you prefer in order to be able to communicate it to your partner. The relationship has to be open to constructive criticism. You have to be able to tell your partner that oral sex needs improving or that you want to try new positions and your partner should be comfortable telling you that you don't last long enough or that your size is an issue. Because after all there are products to fix any sexual issue you may have. But if you don't know there is an issue it can lead to bigger problems in the relationship.

You have to remember that the criticism comes from a positive place and take it for what it is and find ways to move forward and fix the issue. Facing issues like this in a positive way can also strengthen your relationship as a whole because it takes a negative circumstance in a positive direction and this will strengthen that bond of honestly and communication and increase that level of respect between you and your partner because the situation was handled in a respectful manner by both people.

CHAPTER 4

Monogamy in a Sexual World

Monogamy: 1. The practice of marrying only once during a lifetime. 2. The state or custom of being married to one person at a time. 3. The condition or practice of having a single mate during a period of time.

We live in a world full of attractive people and no matter how fine, sexy, or good looking your partner is, you will still notice the other people out there. If you think you're going to be in a relationship and not look at other people you are not being realistic. Our culture makes sure you see each other and encourages you to be seen. Everyone wants to be sexy and be thought of as a "dime". Monogamy is a personal choice that most people make but for some reason they still step out and cheat. Once infidelity enters a relationship it will never be the same. This chapter will talk about the effects of cheating and why people cheat. These are real life situations and answers.

Q: I know you're not talking about FB cheating right now, but when I looked in his inbox he and my friends are flirting with each other.

A: Shit, they are the ones that do it to you, smile in your face all the time they want to take your place. Back Stabbers. See that's why you can't tell your business to them bitches because they know you going through a little something and they try to ease their way on in. I would cut them bitches like they were steaks for playing with me. I'm just saying.

Q: I have been married for two years. We don't have any kids. I'm a registered nurse and I work nights. My husband is at another woman house spending the night while I'm at work. He leaves her place about 4 am to come home so I don't know that he was gone...but I know. One night I had to work and I called my job and told them that I would be running late and I followed him. So I called him and he ignored all my calls. The next day I told him I had called him he said that he had been sleep. He started rubbing and kissing me telling me how much he loved me. It hurt me so bad. It made me hate him. It made me look at him differently as a person. He will never admit that he's having an affair so I didn't even bother approaching him about it. This is my issue, our marriage is over and at this point I don't even want him anymore after what I seen. He has made my heart cold. This is the person that I had planned on starting a family with. I had planned on growing old with him. I could never trust him again. I want to cheat on him to before I end this marriage. I want to make him feel the way I felt. I want him to hurt the way I hurt. I want to do it in his face and be really disrespectful and when he tells me something I want to let him know about the night I followed him. How would you handle this if you were in my shoes?

A: My heart goes out to you. If I was in your shoes I would collect evidence to make sure I was straight when I went to court to divorce his ass. Having sex with someone else will not hurt him. Walking away and chunking up the deuces will make his head hurt. You deserve better.

Q: Hey, I need someone's opinion without being judged. I'm 29 and I meet this guy 26 in Dec. we spent a lot of time together an even took a trip with his family. Our family been know each other for a long time. We belong to the same Church but never really crossed each other paths as adults until then. He is married but they are not together. They got married and he went to work offshore only to come home to an empty house. But it was months later when we hooked up they had been separated. He told her about us and I guess she felt threatened a wanted to work their marriage out. He was with her Christmas Eve and Christmas day. Christmas night he come to spend with me before he left and went back offshore. We was at his friend's house and the door was unlocked she walked in on us having sex Christmas night. (She rode around looking for him because he wasn't answering his phone) Even after she walked in on us having sex Christmas night she still left with him. But I did not know they was even talking about getting back together or he was even with her those days until she walked in on us. But he left with her that night. And we talked about it the next day and I understood him wanting to work his marriage out. Well a month later she leaves him again and knows he back with me. But I'm not feeling it like I was and he still sneaks and talk to her. And she posts status directed at me and had the nerve to inbox me when I posted one back. What am I to do? Cause he is lying an always trying to turn things around on me. I only took him back because I felt like he was a good man and an even better man for wanting to work his marriage out even though the situation could have been handled differently. He says he only talk to her about their divorce but from the stuff she inbox me telling me about us they talk about other stuff. I haven't told him about the inboxing because I don't like to start nothing within my home especially when I feel all I'm going to get is lies an I'm not going to leave. So I refuse to say anything to him about her. Because we live together and I don't want confusion in our house around my two kids.

A: He's not going to leave his wife my love. If it was over when she caught y'all having sex he wouldn't have left with her. If he was going to leave he wouldn't keep going back. He sounds like he really wants to be with her and she really wants to be with him and even with you in the mist they still manage to talk to each other. You need to let him go back to his wife. If he gets his divorce then try and have some type of friendship/relationship with him. If he wants to work on it then let him do just that without you being a distraction. You will be the one hurt in the end. He is her husband let her have her problem back. IJS

Q: Hello, I need your advice on the latest drama in my life. I'm currently involved/ living with a married man. When we met he and his wife were separated, living at different residences. He has since moved into my house. I was told that they were in the process of getting a divorce but it

would be a lengthy process because a minor child is involved. After some time I later found out that they haven't even filed for a divorce yet. Things have really been shaky for us since he accepted a ring from her on their anniversary. He came straight home and told me about. I expressed my feelings yet he still continues to sneak and wear it (on another finger) when he's not around me. I know this because he's occasionally forgotten to take it off. It's gotten to the point now that he just straight out told me he's going to wear it because it doesn't mean anything to him, it's just a piece of jewelry. Am I overacting, which I've been known to do!! Also, he's recently using a social club that he hasn't formally joined yet) as his excuse to leave the house. He's claiming to be going to meetings. Little does he know my ex-boo is a member and keeps me abreast to what's going on, so I know he's lying. I asked him how a meeting went and he got upset and ended up telling on himself. At this point I don't know if it's his wife or another woman. I'm tired of looking like a fool. Am I wasting my time even continuing to deal with him? Is he ever going to divorce his wife? I forgot to include that I've found a condom. He claims it was in his truck when he was cleaning it out and just stuck it in his pocket. Also, she was on side the road sick one night and of course she had their daughter call him. He rushed to her aid. She does know about me and her child is around me all the time.

A: Girl don't be a fool. He's cheating on you for his wife. Some wives don't give up on their marriage. You don't buy a ring for a man if you don't love him and you over him. He still loves his wife, they still having sex, which is not wrong. Having sex with you is what's wrong. He rushes to her aid because that's what he supposed to do as a husband. You have to remember you are the other woman you have to play your role if you plan on staying in this relationship. The sad part is they will be back together, if they haven't filed the paperwork already. Sometimes married people take a break from each other the Bible says that they can do that. It does not say they can start relationships with other people. Throw up the deuces and tell him to go back home.

Q: Hey how u doing?? I have been having a conversation with this guy for about five months now and he has a girlfriend and she lives with him but he says he wants to end it he comes over to my house just about every day morning, evening, and night. Now he wants to stay the weekend with me.. My question is, am I wrong to have dealings with him knowing that he has a girl even though he said he don't want her anymore? We haven't had sex but we came close to it!!! If he continues to cum by I know that it's going to happen because I'm kind of feeling him. What should I do?

A: You don't need me to tell you that you're wrong. You're entertaining a man that is "so say" taken. But go ahead and get it kicked up with him. I will be getting another inbox from you about how he fucked over you for someone else, and he gone tell her how you wasn't on your shit and he wasn't feeling you no more. Men do this shit because y'all let them.

Q: I believe you've met my girlfriend before but anyway we have been dating almost a year. Her ex, whom she calls her baby momma, really gets in the way. It's already enough that my family doesn't accept my choice but she does everything with her ex. The things she does with her she never does with me. She even texts her late at night and I'm like that's rude. It's so much that I can write a book but I love her so much. Just wish her ex would back off. I don't mind her kids because I have a little boy. What should I do??

A: Please stop blaming the EX and put the blame where it belongs. She doesn't really want to be with you because if she did she wouldn't continue to do things she knows will hurt you. The EX don't have to back off she needs to act like she is in a relationship with YOU and leave her EX alone.

Q: I've been trying to help a good friend of mine and I've run out of advice! How much is too much when you're married and your husband has cheated? You suspected it was going on because he was different at times. After doing your own investigation, you find it to be true because of the texts, frequent calls, etc. The female also posts on Facebook (knowing you will see it) whenever they've talked or been together; Also she posts how she means so much to him, the "love" is so strong, he says she's worth the risk, only she doesn't use his name. She has left messages in his voice mail upset/crying if he can't come through for her when she needs him. You have confronted him about this and he has admitted to dealing w/her at one point but denies it now. He has been given a way out where he won't have to lie or sneak around but he says he wants his marriage. Your intuition tells you that there's still SOMETHING but you just can't actually SEE anything! Give me your take on this please.

A: Be there for her as a friend. One thing I know is every woman knows her man. You know when you being fucked over. But this is the thing, that is her marriage and you should pray that God restores what has been broken for them as far as trust. In order for their marriage to work both people have to give 100%. She can't be focused on FB and what the other woman posting. Hoes gone be hoes and she might be messing with more than one married man and that post could be about God knows who. She has to forgive her husband and give him 100%. He has to be willing to be a honest because he is the one who broke the trust. He needs to be 100% honest at all times. All passwords need to be removed, and she has to be able to have access to everything. You have to play your role as a friend I don't believe in telling people to leave their marriage.

Q: I am in a marriage and we both cheat on each other. I know he is cheating on me and he knows that I'm cheating as well. But neither one of us will talk about it, we just act like we don't see the signs. We don't want to be apart because we can't stand to see the other person move on. But while we are together we are not 100% faithful. The guys I deal with know I'm not leaving my home I have too much invested. I just cheat for fun. Most times I'm not even having sex with these men. As for my husband I think it's someone at his job and I think it is sexual because we don't have sex often. How do we stop this behavior?

A: My husband always says in order for a marriage to work you have to have two willing participants. First of all both of y'all do dirt. You both have to agree to end the outside relationships. You both have to forgive each other. You have to talk about what you were getting from this outside relationships. You both have to be willing to move forward.

Q: I am in a relationship with an older man. We both have FB pages. I use to trip about him liking other females photos but now I'm over that. He left his FB page open one day and I went thru his messages and found out that he was talking to females on FB , which isn't a problem , unless the conversation takes a turn. Well, I seen him talking to this one chick and he told her how sexy she is and shit like that. Now let alone they start texting on his phone, but I never knew who she was. I asked him one day who was the number and he told me he don't know. So shit, like any female would do I called the number. We passed a few words, this little bitch told me, "Bitch I wasn't gon' fuck him at first but since I hate little hoes like you Imma fuck his brains out!" Shit, I just told her to get her shine on but after that he stopped talking to the female and shit. Imma say a couple days ago this little BITCH sent a picture of her nasty looking pussy to my man phone. The funny part about it is the BITCH married with kids. I told her to stay away from him and she knows he is taken already. So what do I do about this broad to keep me outta jail??

A: You shouldn't do anything. Why? Because you didn't bring this female into your relationship, he did. If he nips it in the bud then she wouldn't exist. Place the blame where it belongs "on him". He fucked up when they started the whole inboxing thing. Personally I don't believe in the whole female friend "bullshit". I have serious issues with that. But it's not on you to fix this.

Q: Hi I have been in a relationship with a man for going on 6 years he recently moved in together about a year ago and ever since he has been acting up! He lied in told me a girl was his cousin and come to find out she wasn't they were in a sexual relationship I then put a tracking device on his car to try in find out where she lived instead caught him at our managers house at 10 pm after telling me he was going to work! He Denys everything Won't admit to anything even though I've seen proof through his text messages he says I'm crazy and that I'm the only one he messes with like that but yet he's lien about what time he gets off work and disappears throughout the day when I'm at work a d when I ask him where he was he reply's I'm not a child! I don't know what to do I've tried telling him just to leave he wouldn't I do rely on him for financial and emotional support he's really the only person in my life right now! I don't know what to do!!! Or how to make it work! Or to end it!! Help

A: You have all the proof you need. If you stay it's because that's where you want to be. At this point he knows you know but rather than own up to it like a man he calls you crazy. Just know he's not going to stop.

Q: What do you do when you have been in a relationship for 18 years and you have caught your mate cheating on you? You know that you really love this person, but after a few years you seem to not be able to get over. The main thing is you just can't bring yourself to trust them.... It seems you want that experience you went through out of your head!!!!!! But it seems to surface constantly. The mate promised it would never happen again, but again you don't trust or put stock in what they say. However they are good to you most of the time! Part of you wants out of the relationship, but you cannot imagine not having them in your life!!!!!! Again you know you love them, but feel as though you may be falling out of love with them, because the cheating hurt you more than you ever thought it would.. What you do? Or what advice would you give that person? I just don't know what to tell them, because 18 years is a long time and they have built so many good and positive things during this time, but that dam memory of the cheating keeps raising its ugly head! Bring it to me just the way you would handle and you can keep it 100, because when I gave advise I like to be 100, and tell it just like it is! It's only for their good though!

A: I'm not down-playing the pain that cheating can cause. For some people the body goes through the same mental anguish as if someone has died. But you have to ask yourself "How long am I going to keep beating a dead horse?" There are two kinds of people that cheat. Some people are just whores. They always have a wandering eye, they flirt and will fuck up over and over again. Then there is this other person who fucked up one time. They saw the hurt and pain and they caused and really learned from the mistake. When you have a person that really learned from their mistake when the other person is not willing to work on trusting them it only creates wedge in the relationship. People are human and they will disappoint you from time to time. But after being with someone 18 years you know this person in and out. And you should know by now if they have cruel intentions. I'm using the words cruel intentions because if you have cheated and you know how it has hurt the person you love you shouldn't want to do that to them again. Learn to forgive, learn to love that person with your whole heart, and pray that God restores what has been broken.

Q: I think I messed up. I am happily married to the man of my dreams. But he had to go off and do some time for eight months. I have never cheated but while he was gone, I met a guy that is a business owner and he was spoiling me to pieces (he is my brother-in-law's brother). So we started fucking, spending time and shit. I'm not gonna lie, I don't have any feelings because I know it's for a little while. Well, this man started getting mad when my husband would call. He felt like I shouldn't have answered when he's around but I don't care if we're in the middle of fucking. When daddy calls I'm going to answer. Plus, he has found out where I live and I didn't want him to think he can just pop up at my house. I have been dodging his calls, texts and flower deliveries as if I never got them. Now my husband is home and WTF am I supposed to do? Do I need to tell on myself or act like it never happened? Help me!

A: What's done in the dark always comes to the light. You need to put old boy in check and tell his ass to move around because Daddy Home Now. As far as your man is concerned, you could tell him but just know it's going to be one big drama. This is your brother-in-law's brother. Let your man know some shit happened but it was nothing. He is the one you love and old boy was just something to do. Just know once you tell him your marriage will never be the same. Explain to him you was lonely and you fell into the "just friends" trap. Some men that go to jail understand it ain't easy being out here by yourself.

Q: I have been married to my husband for 11 years we have a six year old daughter. I work from 7am to 3:30 pm. I leave home around 6:15am to get our daughter to school, I go to work, get off, I take her to dance, hip-hop, cheer leading and she is also involved in organizations at the church. I make it home around seven pm most days and it is too late to cook so we eat a lot of fast food. Now my husband goes to work at 11am and gets off around 10pm and he works four days a week. When he gets home most times I'm sleep because I get up so early for work. He constantly complains that we don't spend enough time together, I don't cook, we don't have sex enough, but I explain to him I'm one person and I feel like I'm doing it all. All he has to do is go to work. Yes we have the weekends off but our daughter has all types of practices and we have things for church. I felt like I was a good wife and mother but lately he has me second guessing everything. For the last two months he has not asked me for sex at all and that's not normal for him. I really feel like my marriage is going downhill. I don't want to say that he has found someone else but I can feel the change. Help me out.

A: From what I see y'all only have one evening during the week and the weekends that y'all can really spend quality time together. I think it's excellent that you have your daughter in all those activities but I think your husband is feeling neglected. Think about it, when he is home you are gone or sleep. In everything you have to have balance, your child does not have to be in an activity every day of the week. Instead of her being in practice you could be preparing one meal during the week, and one on the weekend. You can even suggest that he prepares one meal a week too. If you are home more then maybe you can get some rest and wake up right before its time for him to get off you can put on some lingerie and get him in the mood. I'm not going to say your husband is cheating but I will say your man wants to feel like he matters in the marriage and you are so caught up on being a good parent you are forgetting to be a good wife. He did the right thing by telling you what he needed and now it's up to you to make the change. Why hasn't he asked you for sex??? Because he already knows the answer. On Friday evenings you should do date night. Get a sitter and let that be your evening to spend time with each other. Sometimes we have to make time for what we want. The not asking for sex is just the beginning.

Q. My husband and I have been married a year and for the most part, we have a good bond. There's just one thing; it drives me crazy when he looks at other women. Literally! It makes my blood boil so much that I become grumpy about everything. I even started taking an antidepressant to deal with my mood! When I tried to talk to him about it, he ends up saying it's just natural, and all men do it. I think that's a load of bullshit. It is significant because it bothers me, makes me feel belittled and ugly. I just need him to understand my side of it. But whenever it comes up, I either get too upset or we get in an argument. Help me!

A: Girlfriend, pull yourself together. You're making drama for yourself. It sounds like you got some issues within yourself. Him looking at another woman can't make you feel ugly unless you feel like that about yourself anyway. What we have to realize is that we all look at other people, even if we want to say we don't. So fucking what he looked at somebody. If she fine, she fine. Hell, tell him, "Yea, she fine as hell". When you do that you take all the power away from him because it doesn't bother you. You're going to run yourself crazy trying to police his eyes. He married you, there will always be someone prettier and finer, that's life.

Q: Ok I have a question. I've been with my guy for three years and we have a beautiful child together, everything was going good until I broke up w/ him a month ago, this was supposed to be a time to for him to get his shit together but he met some little Bitch and now I admit I was a little mad at first but he claim he was just talking to her, I said cool tried to let it go, but I see he is still talking to her, I recently told him I want to make it work. I told him to stop talking her several times to no avail, I want to make this work with my guy but I hate constantly being lied to, I keep asking questions, but he just keeps lying and sugarcoating shit. I also told him to call her n tell her to stop calling him, he said no, she just a stalker what should I do?

A: The reason you broke up with him was to give him time to get himself together. He is showing you that he does not want to get himself together he wants to do what he has been doing. If you don't like him the way he is, he is showing you that there is someone out there who will. Now you have a choice stay or leave. If you are no longer in a relationship he can talk to whoever he wants. He is not going to ask her to stop calling him because he really doesn't want to be with you. He is showing you that in everything he is doing. You need to move on and find what you are looking for, or keep him. Just know he is not going to change.

Q: I'm very attracted to my mother in law. I'm 20. She is a sexy 45 year-old and she has a great body. I know because I have given her massages. From what I have heard she is a freak. How could I get her to have sex with me? She loves when I give her massages. I have given her three of them in the last six months. From her neck to her feet. When I was massaging her legs I went so close to her vagina I felt it on my finger tips and she didn't pull away. I don't want to freak her out because it turns me on to do the massages for her. Any advice for a guy super horny for his mother in law?

A: I know you know your mother in law is off limits and that's all I'm going to say.

Q: I recently decided I'd look through my fiancés phone to see if he was texting a woman that he had been texting once before, (which I know is not right). I confronted him about it, even thought about leaving him, but after we talked it seemed as if the issue had been resolved. Well recently I checked his phone again and it's still going on. Sometimes they even discuss me. He's sending her videos of him jacking off, asking her to send pictures of her pussy, but the thing I don't understand is why, because we have what seems like a healthy sexual relationship? I like to try new things but it doesn't seem like it's enough what should I do?

A: Are you sure you want to marry this man? Just know that if you do this will not stop, it's like you're giving him the go ahead. All men don't need to be in relationships and this is a prime example. At what point did he think about your feelings and how this hurt you? Honestly it's only texting but I know for a fact texting can lead to fucking. And if he wants to see a pussy he should just ask for a picture of yours. Some men get off on the sneakiness and they don't think twice about the person they're hurting. I would tell him I need a break from the situation and when he gets his head right come find me. I would put some shit on his mind because that's just low down.

Q: I have a good woman at home. But I always flirt with other women and sometimes I even have sex with them, but it's just sex, no strings attached. Why do I continue to do this when I know if she ever found out it would hurt her?

A: I was always told "If you want to find a good woman, follow a no good man home". This is about to sound real mean. You just a dog ass man who wants his cake and eat it too. You haven't told me anything this "good woman" ever did you to deserve this. You are selfish. It's your pleasure principle and you are letting it take complete control over you and you don't care who you hurt it the process. She deserves better.

Q: I sometimes have thoughts about having sex with my ex and it makes me not want to have sex with my spouse. I even have dreams about him. I mean he really had me gone. Am I cheating on my spouse? I know that dreams are just expression of how we really feel. But damn! Help me get back focused.

A: The subconscious mind is a like a big memory bank that stores your beliefs, memories and life experiences. This information that is stored in your subconscious mind always affects your behavior and actions in different situations. Do I think you are cheating because you are having dreams, NO! But I do feel that you still have some feelings for that person and you might even miss some of those sexual moments that you shared? These memories are a part of your past. I think it would help if you maybe talked about it with your spouse that way you are not walking around feeling like you are hiding something. I don't think you should feel bad but I do think you should be able to talk to your spouse about anything.

Q: Hey I'm married and love the dick but often fantasize about a good friend who is bisexual as well. How do I confront her about this?

A: Well it sounds like you may have an underlying desire to be with this woman. I run into a lot of married women who are bi-sexual but they suppress their desires because they want to put marriage and family first. If you approach her with it your secret is out. The question is - are you prepared for everything that comes along with this? So how do you approach her? The same way you approach a man. Lay it all out on the table.

Q: I work in an office with a lot of females. There is this one female, she is divorced, with three kids and is in her early 30s, whereas I am in my early 20s. Most of the time, we would talk about family, life, and sometimes sex. She's always telling me about how she would put it on me in a playing way. We are not together but we are cool. We only talk at work and we eat lunch together. I feel myself getting feelings for her and she's not even my woman. I have a girlfriend but I am really digging this older woman. What do I need to do?

A: What you need to do is keep in mind you have a girlfriend. You don't want to get caught up in an affair at your job. You and this woman are clearly flirting with each other but you have to keep a level head. You have to make the choice to separate yourself. If you don't you will fall in the trap that so many people fall into. Do you really want to lose the person who you are with over someone who might not even be serious with you?

Q: I have an issue. I have been married for seven years, been with the same guy for ten years on and off. Well we don't have kids together but I have three kids from two other relationships. Well my two oldest kids dad got out yesterday from jail after being in jail for 12 years and I realized I still love him. I want to be with him but I'm still married. The only reason a broke up was because he had to do a long stretch and he told me to move on and I did that, but night that he is out he wants his family back and is willing to accept my baby girl who's not his child. How do I do this without hurting my husband? What do I do?

A: There is no way you can do this without hurting your husband. You have been with someone for ten years married to him for seven years. You and the kids are a part of his life. You would be wrong on so many levels if you tear your family apart. Don't let your emotions guide you, I promise you will be hurt in the end. Your kid's father hasn't even proven himself, he still has to adjust to society, and he still has to get himself situated. At the end of the day your kid's father will not respect you. You have proven that you cannot be loyal to anyone. See when you loyal to someone you're there for them even when they tell you to leave. When you loyal, you don't walk out on your family that you have built over an emotional feeling that you're having at the moment. He will think if it's that easy to make her leave her husband and I only been out one day. That means she ain't shit. Good Luck in whatever you choose to do.

Q: I have been married for six years. My wife and I dated in college. We have two beautiful kids. Let me start by saying I love my wife. I have been in an affair since last May. I met a girl from work and fell in lust with her. It was wonderful she made me come alive. My wife and I had problems, the main problem was she was focused so much on being a good mother I felt like she didn't have time for me. When she got off from work she would drop the kids off to practice and then she was doing things for the church. I felt like she never had time for me. This girl made that go away, so I thought. It came to a point that I told my wife and she threw me out. It is now October and I want my wife back and my wife wants me back too. But the problem is my girlfriend wants to keep me. I know when I go home I will never see my girlfriend again. I hate that I put both of these ladies in this situation. I really feel like shit, but if I want my family back together I have to do it. I want my family back. I am so stressed. I don't know what to do or where to turn. Please give me your input.

A: Let me start by saying this situation can happen to anyone. No one is perfect and at least you see where you went wrong. First you have to end it with your "girlfriend" and from this point on stop giving her that title because you are a married man. Explain to her that you fucked up and made a bad choice by bringing her into your mess, but from this point you will no longer be communicating with her. I see you said y'all worked together, you might want to see about getting a transfer if that is possible. When you go home to your wife I would suggest y'all attend counseling because things are not going to just fall back into place. Y'all have to talk and understand where y'all went wrong. She has to understand that balance is needed in a marriage. She can do all those things but she still has to have time for her husband. Helping the church is great but you have to take care of home first. Your "female friend" will be ok, this just teaches her not to get into another relationship with a married man cause he wasn't yours to begin with.

Q: I thought I didn't want to be married anymore so I told my wife to leave. Now I want her back but she isn't moving as fast as I want her to. What can I do to speed it up??????
I was dumb and there isn't any other woman worth me losing my wife! Thanks!!!!!

A: Women hold on to words, we remember everything... that's why we fall for men so easily, it's because of all the sweet things you said to make her feel good, to make her feel important, etc. It sounds like you want to be the one to call the shots and you want her to move on your terms. When you bring another woman to the equation that makes things 10x worse. You don't think it hurt her knowing you have been dealing with another woman? it also hurt her when you told her to leave and you didn't want to be married anymore. Put yourself in her shoes. She shouldn't come back so easy you need to put in work. Make her want to come home, and when she gets there you need to talk. What did this other woman give you that made you think the grass would be greener? You should get any and everything you need from your wife. You don't need female friends as a married man that shit only leads to trouble. Be the man that made her fall in love.

Q: I need your advice desperately!!!! I've been seeing this man for almost a year. We're not committed or anything serious, although I would love to be. He's recently been divorced and has stated numerous times how he isn't ready for something serious after being in a serious relationship for so many years. Oh, let me add, his marriage didn't make a year although they were together years before. That's a whole different story though! I really like him and would do anything to be with him, but it's not what he's ready for. Anyway, a couple weeks ago, he spent the night at my house. While he was sleep I decided to roam through his phone and saw that he had been texting another female in which he was flying to go visit the following week. I also went through his email and saw that he has sent flowers to her on three occasions within the last few months. I didn't say anything to him after seeing this. I stopped speaking with him a few days because I was so mad. I couldn't go longer because I missed him so much. So, the weekend he was set to go away he told me he had to work nights at his job. I would make comments to see if he would figure I knew he was lying but he didn't. He continued lying over and over the entire weekend. So, there was a function that I knew he wouldn't have missed had he been home. So, I texted him where he was during the time of the function and he replied sleep for work. When I texted him why he wasn't at this particular function he failed to reply. After a couple hours of no reply, I texted him again, but still got no reply.

So I figured he knew he was busted. The next morning I sent him a text saying I hope he had a safe flight home. Still no reply. A couple days later he texts me like I hadn't texted him a couple days before. I eventually asked why he lied and he said he just did and I don't tell him everything I do or where I go. Although I know the real reason, do you feel I should tell him I went through his phone and know it was a woman he visited the weekend he claimed to be working? I'm hurt he lied, and I hate liars!!!! Although I know where he really was, something in me still wants to see where things could possibly go. What should I do....? Please help!!

A: You are not going to like what I have to say. This man has said he doesn't want anything serious. This is an open relationship, yes you are having sex but it's nothing more. You are both free to do what you like. First of all he is not in a relationship with you so he is not obligated to tell you what he is doing when he is not with you. His focus is with the lady he is sending flowers to and taking a flight to go visit. I guess my question to you is do you not see all of this happening right in your face? Why do you still want someone who doesn't want you back? You want to see where things will possibly go? Here is where they will go - NO WHERE. He does not want a relationship.

EFFECTS OF CHEATING: THE HURT PARTNER'S RESPONSE

When you find out your partner has been cheating on you more than likely you will go into shock, your mind will start racing, you will start to question your relationship and feel like this can't be happening to us. Your thoughts are not clear, and some people start to look at themselves in a negative way.

You lose control over your thoughts. Lots of people start looking at themselves in a negative way for example (jealous, petty, bitter, lonely, ugly). You start comparing yourself to the other woman/man. You are embarrassed, especially if it's a marriage or long term relationship. In a lot of long term relationships the hurt person feels like it's their job to protect their partner's name. You feel like you will never be made a fool of again, you want that person to suffer. Some people even loose the will to live. They can't imagine themselves loving or being loved, some lose the ability to value themselves or their life. You no longer feel like the good woman or man that you thought you were because if that was the case your partner wouldn't have cheated on you.

EFFECTS OF CHEATING: THE UNFAITHFUL PARTNERS RESPONSE

The experience of having two lovers validated you. You may feel desired by two persons, whereas your partner feels loved by none. Even though your partner is suffering, you are experiencing your own definition of HELL. Your secret has been exposed and that is somewhat a relief but now you have another set of problems. Part of you may be drawn to your lover, but another part of you is disgusted because your actions could possibly tear your family apart. The bitterness you felt towards your partner may soften into remorse at the pain you have caused the person that you love. You may decide to give your relationship another chance, only to discover your partner isn't as forgiving as you think they should be. As you are struggling to bring order back to your life, you are constantly reminding yourself that your partner is in no frame of mind to care about your feelings. There are no quick fixes for the type of pain you have because, no magic words. You try and make yourself feel better by justifying your actions. You begin feeling that your needs where unmet and you were forced to go elsewhere to have them met.

SO YOUR PARTNER CHEATED? WHAT'S NEXT?

Once the affair is out in the open you need to decide whether to work on rebuilding your relationship or end it. Don't act on feelings alone. Feelings no matter how intense may be unrealistic. What feels right to you now, you may letter regret. These two options are the worse way to deal with an affair:

- Stay together but never address why the affair happened.

- Stay together with at least one of you continuing to be unfaithful while the other person fights back depression and rage.

When deciding if you're going to let this person continue to be in your life you have to know if this person is good for you.

MONOGAMY FROM A MALE'S POINT OF VIEW:

Monogamy in this day and age is hard. It takes a lot of work to be totally committed to one person in the age of short shorts, tiny skirts and halter tops. It takes two people to move as a unit. Think of it as building a house. Communication is the foundation. This is what relationships build on. Talk to each other and be honest about how you feel. Include your partner in your decision making and allow feedback. This keeps the two of you in agreement. Commitment to each other is the walls of the structure. It allows you to move as a unit. Being committed to each other keeps outsiders from coming into your relationship, outsiders will tear down what you have built together and cause you harm. Trust is the windows to the world. Trust allows you to look out on the storm of nice asses, big breast, and pretty faces but it provides a barrier that doesn't allow that storm to get to you. Respect is that roof over your head. Respect shelters you from that stop on the way home, getting oral sex from a street walker in a back alley or meeting up with that girl from work that says this will be you and her little secret. Respect for yourself and your partner will shelter your form situations like that because you value your relationship more than a quick fling or one night stand. Now you notice there are no doors on the house of monogamy. That's because there aren't any. Communication, commitment, trust, and respect come together to shelter love. Doors are not needed because without them, there can't be any outside influences to come in and interfere with what you and your partner have built. Now with every home you will have up keep cost. The house of monogamy is no different cracks in the foundation communication can cause your whole house to crumble holes in your windows trust can let the element in. It's important to build your monogamous home with the best material because what your put into it will determine what you get out of it.

CHAPTER 5

Open Relationship

An open relationship is an interpersonal relationship in which the parties want to be together but agree to a form of a non-monogamous relationship. This means that they agree that a romantic or intimate relationship with another person is accepted, permitted, or tolerated. Generally, an open relationship is when the parties involved have two or more romantic or sexual relationships occurring at the same time either as a short term relationship, such as dating, or long term relationship, such as marriage. The concept of an open relationship has been recognized since the 1970s. There are several different styles of open relationships. These include:

- Multi-partner relationships - between three or more partners where a sexual relationship does not occur between all of the parties involved.
- Hybrid relationships - when one partner is non-monogamous and the other is monogamous.
- Swinging - in which singles or partners in a committed relationship engage in sexual activities with others as a recreational or social activity.

An open relationship may form for various reasons. These include:

- One partner realizing that they are unable to fulfill the other's needs, varying sex drive between partners.
- One or both partners desiring more freedom, or a variety of sexual partners.
- The enjoyment of new relationship energy, the state of heightened emotional and sexual receptivity and excitement experienced during the formation of a new relationship.

- Being able to meet other couples and individuals with a similar outlook with whom the participants can connect with on an intellectual and emotional level.
- Being in a relationship of convenience, that is, one that is not based on mutual feeling of love towards each other (anymore), but rather on economic or social factors.
- Distance – when partners live in separate parts of the world for part or all of the time.
- Sex may be more pleasing, and the participants may engage in it more frequently than those in an average couple.

Q: *My boyfriend and I are both bisexual. We met at a local gay club. We started out as good friends and then it became more. From time to time we like to have threesomes FFM and MMF. We really enjoy it. My problem is I know that he is attracted to men and I'm cool with that cause I'm attracted to females but I don't like watching him get fucked by another man. I know that he is bisexual but it's different when it's being done right in your face. How do I explain this to him without sounding selfish?*

A: You met him and you both were honest about your sexuality. If it bothers you that bad don't hook up with other people in front of each other. Just tell him you know that he is intimate with a man but it bothers you to see him having sex with a man.

Q: *My boo and I had been talking about having a threesome before we get married. I asked him to find a female, but he tells me to approach the female. I'm not really sure how to go about doing it though?*

A: Most times if y'all are going to a club it's easier if he approaches her, dance with her, buy her a drink, and then tell her what he wants. At that point he introduces her to you and the three of y'all enjoy the rest of the night dancing and drinking. Get her info make plans to meet again. The next time everyone needs paperwork. Y'all enjoy yourself go to a hotel smash. It's done!

Q: *My husband and I just decided to start pursuing an open relationship. We haven't done anything active yet but I did join a couple groups online. There is a man I have been attracted to for about a year now that I want to pursue but I'm not sure what his marital status is and if he's separated from his wife. I know they just sold their house but that doesn't tell me much. That is a whole other issue because I'm trying to figure out how to hint around at him and find out if he's still married or if they are open to that or not . However, the thing is we don't ever see each other. I don't have his personal cell number so I'd have to inbox him or call his office (which I think I'm going to do). My major dilemma is finding someone to get into a relationship with that doesn't just want sex. It seems like the sites I go on are all about sex and I'm not comfortable starting a relationship based on that alone. Please help me.*

A: When you decide to enter an open relationship you are not looking for an emotional connection. It's all physical. So yes in the online groups no one is looking for love. I have a FB group and we have rules and one of them is no handcuffing, and that goes for me and my husband as well. Everyone is fair game. This means you can't get mad because a person talks to someone you are interested in. If you are interested in him his outside life is none of your business. The less you know the better because again you are not supposed to be looking for an emotional connection. All you need to know is if he has a clean bill of health, do y'all vibe, are y'all attracted to each other. Don't bring him to your home, get a room. There are rules to this shit and you have to follow them. You fuck around and let your emotions get involved you're going to be by yourself.

Q: My girlfriend of three years just told me that she thinks she's bisexual and wants to explore sex with other women. I want to be supportive, but the thought of her sleeping with someone other than me (male or female) is too much for me to handle. Should I be supportive?

A: It sounds like she wants to explore her sexuality, she has been wanting to do this for a while. She doesn't think she is bisexual, she knows that she is bisexual and she has that desire right now for another woman and she wants you to be alright with it. Either way she will do it, and possibly do it behind your back. How would she feel if you said, "I think I'm bisexual and I want to sleep with another man"? The question is do you really want to open that door, cause once you open it you can't ever close it back.

Q: I really debated if I should write you this letter to share with your readers. I see so many people saying they want threesomes and open relationships so I have decided to share my story and I hope it helps someone that might be battling with the idea. My husband and I have been married for five years, but together on and off since I was 15, so for about 12 years!! I always knew I liked girls, and had been with them since I was about 16... not a lot, but whenever the opportunity presented itself. My husband's only rule was he had to be present when we were intimate. He eventually let up on that and allowed me to be with girls when he wasn't present as long as I told him about it. We had our first threesome a few years back and it was really fun, and boosted both of our sex drives through the roof until the novelty finally wore off. I told him I wanted him to have sex with her first, to see what it felt like because I thought it would turn me on, but it ended up making me feel weird, until we both had sex with her. We didn't see the girl again. I continued to randomly have sex with my friends on certain rare occasions and would tell him about it. Then one day there was this girl my husband met while working out. It didn't take long to get her in our bed and make her OUR girlfriend. That was about two months ago. I haven't spent more than a couple hours alone with her. It bothers me that he knows her better. In addition, when she comes over, she is more comfortable with him, so they are touching each other, holding hands. The first night she spent the night and was laying on his chest for several hours before I told him it was "time for her to go". Granted, I'm not a cuddlier, so I guess I should be happy that he's getting something from her that he's not getting from me. But I can't help but feel jealous!! My mind races all day thinking, are they spending time together right now? What if he fucks her in the bathroom at the gym, or he goes to her house, or back to our house... is he spending too much time with her and not enough time with me? Is he going to fall in love with her, or will she fall in love with him. He brought me home flowers the other night, and come to find out he did the same for her... he spent money at Victoria Secrets yesterday when I told him I wanted some things from there... and he also bought her stuff too. I can't help but feel like I'm not special to him... even if he says I am, and shows me all that we share together, I still have this deep down feeling in the pit of my stomach that I should be the object of his affection, that I've worked so hard for so many years to obtain that and now this girl is coming in and taking a piece of what was once all mine. I can't shake this feeling that she's driving a wedge in our marriage. I'm always anxious. I try talking to him about it and he tells me I'm reading into it too much, that I need to relax, that he's not going to do anything to jeopardize our marriage and that ultimately this relationship began because I wanted it... which is true. I have learned that open relationships are not all what they are cracked up to be in my opinion. I know I made my bed and now I'm lying in it. I hope this will help somebody.

A: Your husband did everything you asked him to do. He treated her like a girlfriend. You just became jealous in the process. You want the open relationship as long as you are the one getting all the attention. You are selfish. You have two options: 1. Find someone just to have sex with no strings attached, no labels, ya'll just have sex and let that be that. 2. Stop the open relationship lifestyle all together.

Q: I have a question I been with my man for two years and we have some real good sex!!!! Sometimes it's not enough for me. I don't tell him that because I don't want to look like I just want him for sex!!! So I talked him into joining a swingers group in Texas because at times I like to be with a woman and would love to watch him fuck a women in front me. Don't get me wrong I love my man with all my heart and I know he loves me. But we went one night and we had a blast and now all he thinks about is fucking and pleasing me. Do you think joining the swingers club is what we both needed? Please give me your answer because you always keep it real on all your posts!!!! Thank you

A: This is the attraction to swinging.... it's exciting, it gives you an adrenaline rush and increases the level of dopamine transmission in the brain. Dopamine is the "feel good' feeling. You all are still excited from the experience itself. Swinging is just like anything else, it has its pro's and con's. It seems like he only wants to make you happy but you want to make sure you stress to him that he is more than enough to fulfill you. I think after the experience he is always wanting to fuck and please you because he wants to show you that he is more than enough for you. It has been known for swinging to put that spark in people's sex lives but you got to be open minded and you have to set rules.

Q: My husband wants me to have sex with other men. I am an out and out nympho, while my hubby has given up on sex. He tells me he won't mind and wants me to have sex with other men. I'm just dying to do this, but I am worried about the consequences. What would you suggest?

A: Wow..... I am starting to realize that open relationships are very popular, it's just not talked about much. This is an opportunity for you to fill a void you may have been missing for some time. Open relationships are something that many people have a hard time dealing with. So hats off to your husband for considering this option as a way to help meet your needs. It is natural to be concerned about the consequences of moving from a monogamous relationship to a more open one. Communication is key prior to embarking on this new journey. In order to eliminate any concern for negative consequences, any 'rules' around what is acceptable (or not) in your relationship need to be mutually agreed upon ahead of time and respectful to the needs of you both. I would also recommend asking yourself how you would feel if at some point in the future your husband wants to try being with other women. After all, the same rules should really apply both ways. I think you should test just how serious he is by having another man over for dinner. You will have to dress very sexy, and be very flirtatious with a lot of physical contact. Then see what his reaction is, if he gets upset, well then sex with another man would probably not end well. On the other hand it may give you the confirmation you are seeking. If you decide to do it be sure to video your sexual escapade , this might even get him interested in sex again after watching you get fucked good by someone else. Good Luck.

Q: I have a problem. My husband and I have decided to live an alternative relationship lifestyle. I am cool with that. This is my issue - he only wants to bring a female to the bedroom. I don't care about bringing another person into the bedroom I just think I shouldn't be forced to be turned into a lesbian because he only wants females. I'm not into females at all. I really don't care to have sex with them. I would rather him have sex with the female and I should be able to have sex with another man. Please give me some advice.

A: It sounds like he is acting like the average man. If the rules are not fair to both people involved I wouldn't take part in it. How would he like it if you were forcing him to have sex with another man and he wasn't into men? When you get in this type of lifestyle the rules have to benefit both people, or eventually all hell will break loose. You are going to fill entitled to sleep with another man because he gets to sleep with another woman. The difference is when you do it he will say you cheated. My advice is if he is not willing to let you have what you want (a man to fuck you) then tell him you no longer want to take part in it because you are not getting anything out of it, the whole arrangement is only benefitting him and it's not fair.

OPEN RELATIONSHIPS FROM A MALE'S PERSPECTIVE:

There are many reasons people get involved in open relationships. Contrary to what most people think, they are a lot more work than your traditional man and woman duo. There has to be two willing participants in order to enter into this type of lifestyle. This may sound obvious but so many people who agree to enter into an open relationship for all the wrong reasons. They do this because they think it will save their relationship, because they want to please their partner, or pressure from their partner or even cultural pressure. Not to say that they won't be successful open relationships because there is always the possibilities that you may grow to love it. I feel the best way to start this type of relationship is with two people who have a genuine interest in this type of lifestyle. There has to be communication between both people involved and limits within the union. It is very important to be completely honest. Most people in open relationships experience the feeling of jealousy at some point so it is very important to express that through complete honesty to resolve that issue before it starts to creep into other parts of your relationship. The drastic change in intimate surroundings can defiantly change the dynamics of a relationship sometimes for the better, sometimes for the worst. It can improve the sex lives of couples with issues in the bedroom. It can make couples more open and honest. It can bring excitement and adventure. It can also create insecurity, amplify jealousy and cause division. So if you decide to enter into an open relationship do your research and be absolutely sure you are prepared to open this door in your relationship because once you go through it you can never turn back. You can only move forward.

CHAPTER 6

Abuse

There are different forms of abuse and neglect in relationships. Dysfunctional relationships are not normal. Most people stay because they feel like they are stuck in their situation. Abuse can be emotional, financial, sexual or physical and can include threats, isolation, and intimidation. Abuse tends to escalate over time. When someone uses abuse and violence against a partner, it is always part of a larger pattern of control.

Q: My esteem and self-worth took a heavy blow when I was introduced to the unwanted advances of my family members who abused me. However, this physical, sexual and emotional abuse extended beyond blood relatives to include "step" relatives, neighbors and church people. It was as if I wore a target on my little super girl chest that read "Free to do what you like with her". Growing up from a very young age, I had this abusive behavior ingrained in me that I was a living sex toy of sorts. It made me unaware of my value. To this day, I wrestle with being a super success in some areas and a flop of a failure in others. I flop at relationships. I'm always told how great I am but then they always leave. Sexually when a man touches men I feel as if I'm being taking advantage of in a way. Even though I agree to have sex I still get this feeling as if I shouldn't be letting them touch me. What do I need to do to get past this?

A: Sorry that you had to experience abuse on that type of level at such a young age. I have been in your shoes and it does take a toll on how you handle any type of relationship that you encounter in the future. I would suggest you seek counseling because it does help. It's crazy because this type of abuse happens on such a large scale but its never talked about in families and things are always sweep under the rug as if nothing happened. No one ever takes the time to think about the impact that the abuse has on a person they just kind of make you feel like "get over it". I'm not sure if you trust the person you are with to be open with them in the beginning about your past. But that will help them to know how to deal with you. Most people bury that abuse so deep and try and act like it never happened but wonder why they can't bond with anyone. I think you should work on getting help for yourself before you try and enter another relationship.

Q: Together seven years. At the beginning of the year we called it quits and took four months off. He cried for me to come home finally I did. For the first three months back together was amazing. We got engaged and he treated me so much better. Come the fifth month he has decided to go back to his old ways. If he gets free time he says he wants to be with his friends. Days go by and I never get any alone time with him. So I tell him. He then tells me I live a boring miserable life an anything I like is stupid. Then I said I wanted out so he threw my belonging outside. He said when I said I'm moving out he was helping me. Next day its back to I love you like nothing happened. I asked what happened yesterday and he goes you were being a dumb bit**. So after all this I moved out again. He then decided to post on his face book a bunch of things to get people to take his side. (He's 30 by the way and I'm 26) He called me 100 times that day and every name in book. Next day he's calling me asking me to come home. He then wrote on his face book an apology to me. How can one minute he be crazy and then next day it's like hey we can fix and make *this work just come home. He's not bi polar. He now is being beyond nice to me. What do I do??*

A: He might not be bipolar but something is wrong. Going back will only cause the cycle to start over. Get yourself together and move on with your life, you can do better.

Q: I hope you're having a lovely day. Well I'm writing you to ask you your advice about this guy I'm involved with. He's the type of guy that has been thru something in his life or in his relationship that makes him not really share to many of his feelings but he will let you know with the things he does that he cares for you. But he's very insecure. I have a ex-husband and he will accuse me of this asshole every time we get into it it's about him. So I stop talking to him now he is on some other stuff. I love my baby so much I would never cheat on him or be untrue, but he always accusing me. My friend said to find someone and make him jealous. But that's just like cheating but I don't want to do anything to lose him. I'm trying to see if maybe I'm doing something to make him jealous.

A: You are not doing anything wrong. But I will tell you this, be careful about telling your friends about your man because that wasn't good advice that she gave. When a person has been hurt or has been through a lot in the past sometimes they hold on to that hurt. You as his woman have to build him up. You haven't given him a reason not to trust you so when he gets to tripping assure him that he can trust you and that you love him and would never hurt him. I don't know the reason you and your ex-husband are still communicating but if it's not about kids then you might want to limit that communication.

Q: I'm in love with a man who is in love with someone else. We used to work together and flirt with each other. Once I got a promotion I was transferred and we began a serious friendship. We would always talk to each other and he has expressed to me how much he loved his wife, I knew they had financial issues and I found myself always giving him money to help out with something. I knew deep down that as long as I gave him money he would continue to be in my life. We don't have sex because he always has an excuse. I must admit I am jealous of his wife because she has his heart. I'm writing because I need to know what to do to move forward, I have told myself over and over this is the last time I'm giving him money I will not continue to try and buy him but I keep giving him money. I have paid their house note, I have paid for his daughters braces, I have bought countless amounts of clothes, shoes, and cologne. I have paid his mother's light bill, I gave him the down payment for his bike, I have even helped with his wife's tuition. I have invested so much and please tell me how to break this cycle?

A: WOW is all I can say. I can't say that you are being used because you are willingly doing this all because you think your money can move this man. Ask yourself how this relationship is benefiting you. What are you getting out of this? Nothing. This is a married man and personally I believe he and his wife are playing you together.

ABUSE FROM A MALE'S PERSPECTIVE:

In the adult entertainment industry it is rare to find a woman who has never been abused in some way. This is not to say that the adult industry is full of mentally, physically, emotionally, and sexually abused woman looking for love in the wrong places. The reality is every industry is filled with women who have been abused women. Well over half the female population in the U.S. has admitted to being molested. Yes! They have been sexually abused before the age of 13. Not to mention the portion of the female population that has been mentally and physically abused. So I think it's safe to say the chances of entering a relationship with an abused woman are highly likely. These are disturbing facts but it made me realize a few things about us, meaning men in general.

First of all, we need to reframe from being filthy; nasty sexually deviant motherfuckers! Unless it's with a consenting adult. Yes this is a touchy subject that most people want to stay away from because of the pain and negativity that oozes from it. But from the staggering high rate in the statistics I feel it needs to be talked about. More than likely you have a friend or relative who is an abuser or molester. Face it! If over half the female population has been molested then the number of men engaging in this behavior is just as big.

Parents have to communicate with their children an early age. Explain to them about inappropriate touching. Let them know that it's ok to tell if someone has touched them or said something to them that made them feel uncomfortable. And if you find that your child has experienced the trauma of being taken advantage of do not ignore it and think that it's just going to go away. The pain of being abused never goes away. It's like the death of a close relative. A child's innocence has been lost and it will never return. They will need counseling to deal with the pain, confusion and shame that comes along with being abused. They will need to learn ways to cope and function normally in society through all the pain that they harbor in their minds and hearts. They also need to be assured that it's not their fault, that it shouldn't have happened and that every step is being taken to move them into a safer and secure environment so they won't have to worry about experiencing that ever again. What people don't understand is that there are lifelong effects that people who have been abused endure. They have intimacy issues, problems asserting themselves into society, trust issues, self-esteem issues, relationship issues and the list goes on and on.

If you are an adult who has been in an abusive situation, you should get counseling to help you work through the issues that stem from that experience. You will never forget. But you have to get to a place in your life where the pain of what happened to you doesn't enter into your everyday life with the people who love and genuinely care about you.

If you find yourself in a serious relationship, sit down with your partner and talk about it with them. I'm not saying that you should go through all the gory details of the situation. Just be honest and upfront about what happened so that they can get a better understanding of who you are now. Give them an idea of how they need to help you progress in the life recovery from things that were done to you against your will. You partners may not understand why you like to keep the lights off when you're being intimate or why hugging others makes you uncomfortable. Give your partner the opportunity to be able to understand you completely so that you can move forward on a stronger footing in your relationship.

Now to the men and woman who engage in physical, mental and sexual abuse. You have a sickness. It may stem from abuse. It may be caused by mental illness. It may be from watching your father take is boot to your mother and you thinking "hey I don't like this but she's still with him so it must be ok". Whatever the case may be you have a problem. You need to seek professional help. You need to get to the core of the issue. Why do you say such mean things to the person you decided to spend the rest of your life with? What are the triggers that make you hit the person you say you love? What the fuck is in your mind that allows you to find your eight year old niece sexually attractive. Only you can unlock the answers to these troubling questions. You have to look deep into the murky thoughts of your mind and ill will in your heart for answers. You have to understand our children are our future. They deserve to be guided in the right direction and sheltered from all hurt and harm because they didn't ask to be here. Women are our backbone. They deserve to be treated equally with love and respect and admiration for putting up with all the bullshit we throw at them. Men are supposed to be leaders. Providing and protecting every step of the way. If man can get his act together everything else will fall into place. Then we will be raising generations of young men who respect their mothers and sisters, who grow up to become providers and leaders.

Young women who get the respect and admiration they deserve growing up believing they can do and be anything they want to be in life. Men will have wives who trust them and their word to do what's best for their family and will be there by your side to the bitter end. And men can enjoy the day that the word "MAN" actually stands for something powerful and positive and not just the three letter word we use for males over the age of 18 today. But change starts with us.

CHAPTER 7

Fetish and BDSM

The term "Bondage" describes the practice of Physical restraining. Bondage is usually, but not always, a sexual practice. Bondage means binding the partner by tying their appendages together; for example, by the use of handcuffs, sashes, or by lashing their arms to an object.

The term "Discipline" describes psychological restraining, with the use of rules and punishment to control behavior. Punishment can be pain caused physically (such as caning), humiliation caused psychologically (such as a public beatings) or loss of freedom caused physically (for example, chaining the submissive partner to the foot of a bed).

In a BDSM relationship the partner who has the active role in a session or in the entire relationship is described as the "top", a role that often involves inflicting pain, degradation or subjugation. The partner referred to as the "bottom" submits voluntarily to the actions of the top.

BDSM practitioners sometimes regard the practice of BDSM in their sex life as role playing and so often use the terms "Play" and "Playing" to describe activities when they are in their roles. Play of this sort for a specified period of time is often called a "Session", and the contents and the circumstances of play are often referred to as the "Scene".

Sadomasochism refers to the aspects of BDSM surrounding the exchange of physical or emotional pain. Sadism describes sexual pleasure derived by inflecting pain, degradation, humiliation on another person or causing another person to suffer. On the other hand, the masochist enjoys being hurt, humiliated, or suffering within the consensual scenario. Pain and pleasure are so closely related. Pain, just like pleasure, releases endorphins, the compound connected to pleasure and enjoyment. Obviously, this style of sex can be very heated and passionate, part of why people enjoy engaging in it. The post important part is to stay safe.

The first thing you need to do before starting BDSM is create safe words. Although pain does release endorphins during sex, you will still experience pain, and sometimes it can be too much. I recommend creating a safe word you never use during sex, like "yellow" or "brownies." When you here the safe word this means to stop.

The most common way to start is spanking the buttocks during sex, simply because it doesn't make sense to start with another body part. Spanking releases endorphins through the body and is easiest during the doggy style or cowgirl positions for heterosexual couples. Most times people are participating in a BDSM style of sex and don't even realize it. Lol

Q. I am a single Black male who has recently experienced strap on sex with a dominate female and I enjoyed it so much now I want more. I would like to know how can I find an understanding enough female that would also enjoy this type of sex. Such a taboo subject would mark me as homosexual are a down low brother which is the farthest from the truth in my case, cause I have zero attraction to men never have. I prefer to keep my bedroom behavior private and am not into the internet dating sites. So any tips on how I can possible find a female that is into that and is also open to a relationship? I would also like to remain anonymous

A: Thanks for being so open with me. Honestly you have to find a person that views sex openly and that person has to understand that satisfaction has nothing to do with sexuality and sexual preference. Just like I understand that you enjoy deep penetration to stimulate your prostate there are other females who understand the same thing. Most females wouldn't want to use a strap on the first time but you can work up to that level. I have married couples that shop with me all the time for a strap-on. To find a female this open will take time. We live in a world that thinks everything is Taboo. I wish you the best of luck and more than likely a bi-sexual non judgmental female would be your best bet.

Q: This is a question of etiquette. I am considered to be a submissive in my relationship. My lover has requested that I wear a butt plug all day for him. He would like this to be a normal day. However, I hold a high level position at my job which requires me to attend meetings, often several times a day. While I want to do this for him, I'm concerned that this is disrespectful to my colleagues. Obviously, no one else will know, but I will. What do you think?

A: I think you have to be comfortable with the whole idea. You say you want to do it for your lover, and it is great to try things out for each other, but you have to be comfortable with doing it for yourself otherwise it's just not worth it. If you're not, and your main concern about your disrespecting your co workers is too big to overcome, find a way to engage with your lover that works for both of you. My only concern is that the lubricant you need to use to insert it will dry up throughout the day, so when you take it out you are more likely to injure yourself. If you are going to wear it all day be sure to take it out and reapply lube every time you got to the restroom.

Q: I slept with my boyfriend for the first time about two months ago. He went down on me and suddenly, without a warning he slaps me right between my legs. It did not really hurt, so I didn't say anything but like 30 seconds later he does it again. It didn't hurt but it didn't feel nice either. So I asked what he was doing and he said he was bringing the freak out of me. He called me a trashy bitch. I was like oh shit! I was in a state of shock because I have never experienced anything like this. Is this type of sex common? If yes, why? What do you get out of it? I mean I can kind of see why you would slap a girls butt, but her vagina? And call her ugly names in the bedroom? He has toned it down some. He says he's going to take it slow with me because he almost ran me off.

A: This type of sex is called BDSM. He gets off by humiliating you. Don't take it personal. Think of it as role playing. He is just trying to show you how to please him. Sex is different for every person and nobody does it the same. I bet he would really get off if you started talking shit back to him. Tell him to fuck your trashy pussy. And tell him how you have been such a dirty bitch and he needs to spank your pussy. That will get him going. Let me know how it works out for you.

Q: Hello again! Another question, and I'm really curious to hear what you think I this. So a good friend of mine and I were chit chatting, just our usual girl talk about sex. And she tells me that even though she considers herself a heterosexual female and is in love with her husband, she has a fetish for gay porn. She likes guy on guy. She masturbates to it and finds herself fantasizing about it during sex on the regular. She finds it so arousing to watch. Is this normal? Or I guess the right question would be, have you ever heard anything like this?! I personally was caught off guard with it and I consider myself pretty open minded! What do you think?!

A: Wow. Nothing seems to amaze me anymore but this question just took me fast. Most fetishes are not normal. If it was normal then it wouldn't be a fetish. It's no different than people that like feet or like being pissed on. And this one is a first. I have heard of ladies liking lesbian porn but never male on male.

Q. My wife and I have been married for 12 years and we have three children. We are still very much in love and I think we are very good friends as well. I try to find time to massage her feet and legs each night, sometimes for an hour or more. I also give her oral sex, day or night, whenever she requests, I continue until she tells me to stop, which is usually no more than five minutes because that is all she wants. We have intercourse whenever she wants, which is usually several times a week. Once a week she allows and expects me to cum, always inside of her so as to maximize her pleasure. She likes to tease and deny me orgasm, and occasionally enjoys giving me oral sex. We have agreed that our sex life will be at her discretion and her choosing, and that I will cum only when she chooses. But she only lets me cum maybe once a week. How do I change this?

A: It sounds like you two have established a practice known as erotic sexual denial, a form of teasing where one person uses sexual stimulation to bring another to the brink of orgasm. Right before they're about to climax, stimulation is removed. Orgasm denial creates sexual tension and intense excitement, but it can also result in psychological dependence on the partner who's in control. "Letting sleeping dogs lie'" is a passive way of dealing with this situation. You need to let her know you want to cum more often. You are having sex several times per week and you want to enjoy it to.

FETISH FROM A MALE'S PERSPECTIVE:

I think the word fetish has a bad rap. Sex is about gratification. A fetish is a fixation on an object or body part. Face it, most men have a fetish for a nice ass or a big perky set of double D's. It is part of what attracts us to our partners and what we need to get aroused. There are many types of fetishes. Animate fetishes involve body parts. Form fetishes involve the shape of objects for sexual arousal. Media fetish involves the textures such as silk, lace, and latex. Just to name a few, fetish can be nearly anything. The most importing things in my opinion to focus on if you have a fetish, which you probably do, is to be honest with yourself about it. Be comfortable with it and be up front about it with your partner. The last thing in the world you want to have with your partner is a fucked up sexual relationship. That is a definite relationship ender. As long as you are within the confines of the law with is very importantly because there are people who have fetishes that may not be legal. And you are comfortable with your own sexuality you can have a very healthy fun and exciting sex life. A fetish is nothing to be ashamed of. Be true to yourself and embrace your sexuality.

CHAPTER 8

How To Questions and Answers

HOW TO SQUIRT

STEP 1: Maneuver your fingers to find her g-spot. Slide your fingers in about two inches, UP, and then BACK towards the front of the pussy (like you're going up behind her clit.) You should feel, on that wall, a very rough patch of skin – rougher than the rest of her smooth inner pussy. You've found it! That's the G-SPOT!!!!!

STEP 2: As you start to press/pull your fingertips against the g-spot, she should start getting wetter. If you're doing it right, and she's comfortable with it, you'll start to hear squelching, sponge-like sounds. The g-spot is like a sponge. It contains a lot of liquid, and feels rough. Keep pressing your fingers against it, over and over.

STEP 3: When she gets close to ejaculation, she will say that she needs to pee. SHE DOES NOT NEED TO PEE. It's just a temporary sensation that will pass, but you have to make sure she knows about it beforehand. Hold her legs apart with the other hand, if you have to. You can even use your head or knees or whatever to hold her legs open, but make sure she stays relatively still (or she might get hurt on your fingers) and that you KEEP GOING. In fact, when she needs to pee, that's when you should start doing it harder, because orgasm is around the corner.

10-50 seconds after the pee sensation begins, she will start to cum. When she does DON'T STOP. Just do it harder and harder and harder, pressuring the g-spot upwards all the while. Now she should start to ejaculate. She'll scream, and her pussy will start shooting clear (transparent), odorless liquid all over the place. There could be a lot of it, it might soak you completely and soak the sheets and everything around her so make sure you're prepared.

Q: When a female "squirts", what is the liquid that comes out? Is it urine? I've read up on it, but can't seem to get a definite answer.

A: Squirting refers to a watery fluid that originates in the G-Spot and is secreted by the Skenes/Paraurethral Glands through the urethra before and/or during orgasm. Although the fluid released during female ejaculation comes from the urethra, rest assured it is not urine. The fluid is female ejaculate, and it comes from the ducts around the urethra, not from the bladder, where urine is stored. The reason why people may confuse female ejaculate with urine is due to the fact that female ejaculate can also sometimes travel back up into the bladder, which is called retrograde ejaculation. And because the female ejaculate may mix with urine and even share some of the same properties of urine - urea and creatine. Many people think that it is urine; however this is not the case.

Female ejaculate is also distinctly different from normal vaginal fluid. Normal vaginal fluid can vary in taste, smell, color and consistency depending on the menstrual cycle, hormonal levels, food intake, presence of infection etc. Female ejaculate on the other hand is fairly consistent in the taste, smell, color and consistency. It is a sweet smelling, watery type of fluid and is not the typical fluid that one sees when a woman is wet from sexual arousal or having had an orgasm.

During sexual arousal the G-Spot becomes enlarges and the tissue surrounding the urethra becomes engorged with blood and the Skenes/ Paraurethral glands begin to produce and fill with fluid. The pressure rhythmic from fingers or toys or a penis, or the contractions of orgasm pushes the fluid out through the urethral opening causing ejaculation.

The amount of fluid expelled during ejaculation can vary from woman to woman however the average amount is somewhere around two tablespoons, this can be affected by how hydrated a woman is, how much she pushes while ejaculating.

Q: About the G spot squirting situation, is that something a woman can try on her own to see if it works before she lets her man do it?

A: First empty your bladder before doing this. Get yourself aroused as you normally would. Masturbate for a while, and then begin. The clitoris probably holds the key to female ejaculation for most women. If the clitoris is not stimulated a woman is less likely to become highly aroused. If she is not highly aroused, her paraurethral glands will not fill with fluid. If her paraurethral glands are not swollen she may not have a G spot orgasm. So before you can go exploring for the G spot orgasm you must master clitoral stimulation beforehand. The best way to stimulate your G spot is with a dildo that has a curve near the tip or a stimulator called a flicker. If you use the dildo insert it and keep hitting that spot until you feel like you have to pee. If you use the flicker say on the clit until it gets hard and starts to stand up like a dick.

When you are about to ejaculate, you will get the feeling to need to pee (this is normal, as both fluids come from the same place). This is because both urination and ejaculation require a woman to be able to let go and relax her bladder sphincter and her pelvic muscles. If you keep your bladder sphincter closed and tighten your pelvic muscles, you cannot urinate or ejaculate. Women who want to ejaculate are advised to push out when the urge to urinate or ejaculate comes over them at the point of orgasm. Doing this gives your body permission to ejaculate. Do not fight the urge; go with the flow, literally. Relax and breathe deeply. A slow build up, with lots of teasing, may help produce the greatest urge and strongest orgasm. When orgasm occurs, relax your bladder and press out as if urinating. If you ejaculate you will likely feel a new and strong sensation, if not, you will still experience a strong orgasm, so nothing is lost. Make sure you have towels and plenty of them. I hope this helps.

HOW TO SUCK DICK REAL GOOD

About 15min of you doing it like this:

1. First you need to get him turned on - be more aggressive, grab his stuff, slowly massage his balls through his pants, it's important that you act as seductive as possible - the more you're turned on - the more he'll be turned on. Pull his pants down slowly and act as naughty as possible - this is a great turn on.

2. Grab his hand and lick on his fingers slowly before you give him head - just put his middle finger slowly into your mouth and suck on it, up and down, slide it slowly and moan - you have to moan a lot so he feels like a king.

3. As you're licking one finger, slowly start stroking his shaft (penis) with your other hand, you have to be on your knees and he should be standing, look him in the eyes - this way you can see his reactions. You need to love giving him head if you want him to really enjoy it.

4. Most girls make the mistake of being too soft - don't do that, grab his penis tightly and stroke it hard, as you're twisting his shaft with one hand slowly start sucking on the head (the tip) of his penis, curl your tongue around it, twist it in circles, then point it upwards and slowly lick it while you're watching him.

5. Say something like "mmmmm I love it" then smile, smiling is very important - it conveys that you love it. Keep on stroking and sucking harder.

6. Start talking dirty to him, put your hands around his balls and tickle them gently - make sure you are gentle 'cause his balls are very sensitive, as you're tickling, keep on stroking and sucking.

7. Once you see that he's getting closer start stroking harder - and don't even think about slowing down. Scream at him, tell him you want it - tell him where you want it (swallowing will make him go crazy just as you want it) - then as he starts to come, you have two options - you can hold his penis or he can hold it - I suggest you let him hold it and squeeze it out.

8. Then hold his penis and stroke it slowly, just as if you were trying to squeeze every last drop out of him into your mouth, give it a few more finishing licks.

9. Then smile at him, open your mouth and show him what you've got in your mouth, smile, then swallow all of it - then look up at him again and open your mouth to show him it's gone.

10. Smile again, believe me he'll love you for it.

HOW TO DEEP THROAT: HOW TO GET HIM ALL THE WAY DOWN

Neck angle is everything. Sitting as you are now reading this, if you keep your shoulders still and push your head forward your neck is at the perfect angle. You can of course tilt your head up slightly, to get the same angle but I've always found pushing my head forward is the best way for me and it really opens up my throat. It is trial and error getting it spot on. When you deep throat a lot you'll find you can take him easily in any angle, but to begin with OR if you haven't done it for a while, the part under your chin that needs to drop down in order for him to fit, becomes tight and therefore its' more difficult to do.

Your Tongue: Try to keep your tongue flat. The tongue has a tendency to want to curl up at the back of your throat, it's all part of being nervous. But this will really make you gag. In the beginning I used to poke my tongue right out of my mouth. I also used to widen my mouth just before I breathed out and went down. Widening your mouth is very similar to yawning. Your mouth widens and your lips pull back at the sides too (hopefully that makes sense). Breathe all the way out, and open as if to yawn to the point where you can feel the sides of your mouth and jaw stretch. You can notice that when you do it, you throat does widen for a second a split second after you fully open your mouth. Keep doing it until you feel it, you will feel it. (Remember not to draw air in) When you have him in your mouth, slide him to the back, and when you are just about to go over the gag area, widen like a yawn without breathing in.

BREATHING AND DEEP THROAT

You can still breathe with the tip of him in your throat, but once the throat drops you cannot breathe in or out. It very important that you breathe OUT before you go down. An endoscopy Doctor (and friend) explained to me that part of the Gag reflex is the LUNGS expelling air in a rapid way. This stops the contents from your stomach going into your lungs. During deep throat this happens a lot. In fact this happens far more frequently than gagging from the stomach. Essentially what you do is to draw air IN through the sides of your mouth as you come up and breathe out through your nose as you go down.

Q: I'm not used to giving blow jobs to my friend guy. How can I give him the ultimate head job that makes his toes curl. Please HELP!!!!!

A: Make your tongue as flat as possible (it'll cover more territory that way), then slowly run it along his shaft from base to tip. Take your time, leave no spot unlicked. Next, place a Candy Cock Ring around the base.... Then nibble a few so that your mouth gets all minty and cool. Start to suck the head and then pull it out and blow on it. This will make his toes curl. Giving a good head job is all about stimulating him. You can use Dickalicious. It is an arousal cream that stimulates the nerves in the dick. You also have to be confident and know before you start that you are "The Best".

HOW TO HAVE ENJOYABLE ANAL SEX

Step 1. Use a Fleet to clean yourself out. You can also use a little baby oil, because it is guaranteed that everything will be cleaned. Of course put the baby oil inside the enema. Take a bath or shower.......

Step 2. You will need Anal Ease and Lubricant. If you have a lube shooter great if not that's ok. Let him put some anal ease on his finger and insert it in your butt. You will feel this but it shouldn't hurt. At this point he should NOT be trying to insert himself in. Continue with your foreplay.

Step 3. Use lots of Lubricant (I recommend Astroglide or Soothe) both or great for Anal Sex. At this point your partner can start to enter slowly. You have to relax, and he has to go slow. At some point the Anal Ease will wear off but that's ok because by that time your body will have opened up.

Q: Have you ever had an anal massage? The anal area has many nerve endings and can be a wonderful addition to a sexual massage. It does not mean you will have to have anal sex, it just means you are willing experience this new pleasure.

A: Use a latex glove and some anal lubricant. The walls of the anus and vagina are thin. Beyond the very sensitive entrance of the anus you should be able to feel her G Spot through the wall of the anus. Take your other hand and gently massage her clitoris.

HOW TO DO A DIRTY 360

Sex tip for the grown and sexy: Do a Dirty 360. Get into girl-on-top, and spin all the way around without pulling the penis out of you. Have you ever done a 360? If so, please share your tips for making it work.

Males can do a 360 as well: Your man lies on top of you, entering you in traditional missionary style, but then he starts doing a 360-degree spin, all the while keeping his penis deep inside of you. As he's rotating and thrusting, help guide him around your body like a propeller would spin around the top of a helicopter. Make sure to lift his legs when they swing around over your head.

Q: I would like to use food (preferably sweets) during sex. How do I do this without it getting too messy? Am I weird for wanting to do this?

A. You are not weird; you just want to have fun during sex. Using food during sex goes back to the ancient Romans and Greeks, who staged grape-eating orgies. There are many creative things you can do with food. Get you some pineapple rings in the can. Drain the juice (drink it lol) put the pineapples in the freezer to chill them fast. Next you use the pineapple slices for a game of "ring toss" then eat the pineapples off him. Then give him some head he will never forget. Did I mention how good he will taste? Lol.

First, put a sheet (or two) on the bed that you don't mind messing up. To start off, you can put peppermint schnapps into each other's belly buttons for body shots. (Then blow on it.)

For something more sensuous, take turns pouring Hershey's Chocolate Syrup on each other, then licking it off. You can try it cold or heat it up and drip it on each other. Once the syrup has cooled down, dip his penis in bowl of it for a new twist on oral sex. (It's called a "Mr. Goodbar.") Have him pour the chocolate sauce on you from the mouth down and then lick his way to (your) orgasm. You'll never look at Hershey's Chocolate Syrup the same way again.

Other foods to use include jelly, honey, and old-fashioned whipped cream. After you are done, take a shower to wash off the sticky goo. (Make sure you wash your vaginal area well, as sugar in there can cause a yeast infection.)

Also interesting is pouring champagne on each other before oral sex. Altoids can be used for some "minty fresh" oral action -- and candy "pop rocks" feel really bubbly.

Tip: Oral Sex with cold grapes in his mouth. For one it's going to be juicy and taste really good. But his mouth will be cold. If he is really bold he should play around the anal area with the grapes and lick that ass.

HOW TO MOVE ON AFTER A BREAK UP

Q: You give great advice, so here it goes. I have been with my husband for 17 years. We recently separated about three weeks ago. Since the separation, he has gotten involve with his high school love. If I call him, he is there. He will not speak of the girl or even fully admit that they are a couple unless he's trying to hurt my feeling at that present moment. My thing with the separation is, he's living in dreamland while I'm crying, not eating, and not sleeping. It seems that our 17 years was only 17 minutes. This pain that I have in my heart hurts like hell and I need to let go, but how do I?

A: I'm not sure what brought on the separation but I need you to get focused on you. You have to heal for yourself and kids. As you can see he is moving on and trust me, men think the grass is greener but when they really look at it.... It's still grass. He knows that this is hurting you. Stop calling him, completely ignore his ass, don't play house with him, don't treat him as your husband keep it strictly on a level about your kids. When you get married it's easy to lose yourself, get you some hobbies, get some friends, go out and keep yourself busy. If you don't have a church home find one. It's going to take lots of prayer. I'm not saying don't love your husband or pray for your husband. I saying focus on Yourself for a change.

Q: Good Morning!!! I hope you can explain something to me. I didn't know woman could have wet dreams Is that possible? Well last night I had a dream that I was having sex with another man (my EX) which I am well over no questions no doubt. I could hear myself moaning in my sleep is this normal???? So when I awaken my bed was soaking wet as if I had pissed on myself why is that?? And how do I explain this wet bed to my husband???

A: Most people experience Wet Dreams when they are young adults. A wet dream is a type of spontaneous orgasm, involving either erection and/or ejaculation during sleep for a male, or lubrication of the vagina for a female. It is possible to wake up during a wet dream, or to simply sleep through it. We dream because of the intense activity that is constantly going on in our subconscious minds. And since sex is one of the most powerful of all human drives, it's not surprising that so many dreams have a strong sexual content. If we have deep urges to do certain things, they are highly likely to come out in our dreams where our consciences cannot prevent them happening.

Q: Please keep my name out should you post. Do you have any suggestions on how to ride a man for those of us who feel like we don't know what we are doing?

A: I never release names. The most important thing to remember when riding is not being afraid to move. Communicate with your partner. Ask him if he likes how it feels. Don't be afraid to touch his chest, pinch his nipples, or stroke his nuts. Bounce, grind, roll, ride the head of his dick. Put your legs in different positions try Froggy style, get on your knees, sit on it with your legs on your shoulders. Keep in mind he needs to be participating too. He needs to thrust that dick inside you, slap your ass, suck your titties. Y'all have to do what feels good.

Q: I was wondering about the depth of the vagina. I've read statistics that say that the average vagina is only three to four inches deep. This seems way too small to me, since the average penis is considerably longer than that. Wouldn't that mean that most penises would crash into the cervix repeatedly during intercourse? Since this obviously doesn't happen, my question is this: does the vagina actually elongate during intercourse to accommodate the entire length of the average penis?

A: Yes, just as the vagina has the capacity to expand, allowing for the passage of a baby during childbirth, the vagina also has the ability to become longer during sex to accommodate a penis. As you mentioned, for some women, the depth from the vaginal opening to the tip of the cervix is three to four inches when they are not sexually aroused. When a woman is aroused she may have a vaginal depth of five to seven inches. Regardless, during arousal, blood flows to the genital area, and sexual excitement causes the upper two-thirds of the vagina to lengthen by forcing the cervix and uterus to move upwards. The vagina also lubricates to help ease penetration. Some people think that the vaginal canal is a continuously open space. However, this is a misperception. Think of the vaginal canal as if it were a balloon that is not filled with any air. The walls, which have the potential to expand and elongate, gently touch one another. When something is placed inside, they mold around the width and accommodate the length of a penis, tampon, finger(s), or sex toy. Sometimes during penetration, a penis or other object inserted in a vagina does hit the cervix. This may be an indication that the woman is not aroused enough; when she is more aroused, her vagina will expand and her cervix, the neck of the uterus, will lift up and move out of the way.

Q: How do you know when your vagina needs to be tightened?

A: Some women have a problem with loose vaginal walls or a loose vagina opening. This can frustrates them or their intimate partners due to lack of sensation when having sex. While some women can easily tell that their vagina is loose, some women cannot. Here are some ways to help determine whether you have a loose vagina:

*The need to insert bigger objects into the vagina for stimulation and arousal

*The difficulty to grip your index finger using your vagina

*Your vagina no longer closes when you are not turned on

*You can freely insert more than three fingers without much resistance

*Difficulty to achieve orgasm

*Failure to satisfy your partner unlike before

Q: So how do you tighten up the vagina walls? I know there's sex creams but I'm talking about like exercising. What type of exercises helps this?

A: It takes diligence to identify your pelvic floor muscles and learn how to contract and relax them. Here are some pointers: Find the right muscles. To identify your pelvic floor muscles, stop urination in midstream. If you succeed, you've got the right muscles. Perfect your technique. Once you've identified your pelvic floor muscles, empty your bladder and lie on your back. Tighten your pelvic floor muscles, hold the contraction for five seconds, and then relax for five seconds. Try it four or five times in a row. Work up to keeping the muscles contracted for ten seconds at a time, relaxing for ten seconds between contractions. Maintain your focus. For best results, focus on tightening only your pelvic floor muscles. Be careful not to flex the muscles in your abdomen, thighs or buttocks. Avoid holding your breath. Instead, breathe freely during the exercises. Repeat three times a day. Aim for at least three sets of ten repetitions a day. Don't make a habit of using Kegel exercises to start and stop your urine stream. Doing Kegel exercises while emptying your bladder can actually weaken the muscles, as well as lead to incomplete emptying of the bladder — which increases the risk of a urinary tract infection.

www.ingramcontent.com/pod-product-compliance
Lightning Source LLC
Chambersburg PA
CBHW071756090426
42737CB00012B/1843